The GIRL GUIDE Annual

Published by special arrangement with
THE GIRL GUIDES ASSOCIATION

Edited by Robert Moss

Purnell

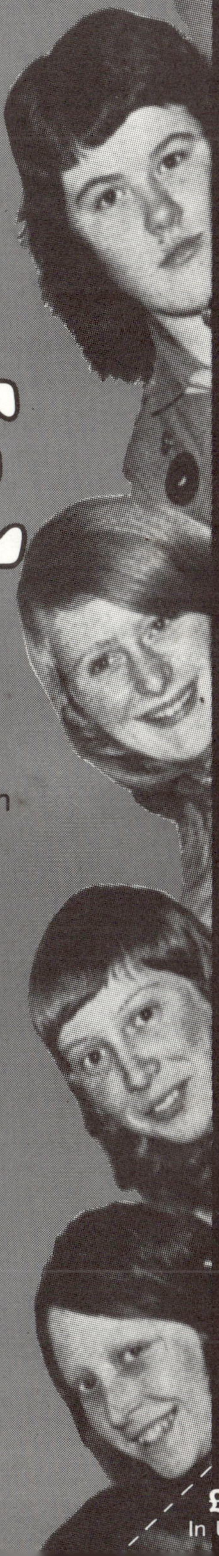

£1.95
In U.K. only

Badges Galore

Some time ago I made a doll,
Because I like to sew,
Then knitted her a set of clothes
Just like an Eskimo.

I took her with me to a test,
Toymaker Badge, part two,
Then used her for the Knitter Badge,
And Needlewoman too.

I learned about the Commonwealth
For yet another test,
And took for section number four
The doll that I had dressed.

I read a book on Canada
And wrote full many a line,
And very soon the Reader Badge
And Writer Badge were mine.

I gave a talk for Speaker Badge
On Canada, no less,
And showed my doll to illustrate
How some Canadians dress.

I did some cooking out of doors
For Camper Badge last year,
Which helped me with my Hiker test,
Backwoodsman and Pioneer.

I have a sleeve of badges now
And wear them all with pride.
One learns so many useful things
When one becomes a Guide.

Perhaps I chose an easy route,
But having reached my goal
I now have time to concentrate
On leading my Patrol.

by Eileen Chivers

Map Reading Quiz

by George H. Haines

(All details relate to the latest 1:50,000 issue of the Ordnance Survey maps)

How are these shown on the latest O.S. maps?

1. What information does the map give about churches?
2. What are the signs in the photograph? They are seen on walls and in other places.
3. How are national parks shown on the map?
4. What is the odd feature about the heights and contour lines on the map?

What are these signs?

5. What does the map tell you about ferries?
6. How are the sites of battles marked on the map?
7. What does the map tell you about beaches?
8. How does the map help you to find popular places for sightseers?
9. The National Trust owns much land in Great Britain. What does the map show about National Trust properties?
10. Power lines cannot be missed in the country. How are they shown on the map?

The Trail of the Missing Jelly

by A. I. Duncan

There was no break in the good weather, and the 2nd Dundela Guide Company's annual camp continued to be a great success. The six members of the Forget-Me-Not Patrol were busily engaged in tying up their bedrolls in time for morning inspection.

"Now, Shelagh, isn't it much better to know what you are about when you come to camp instead of having to learn at camp?" asked Caroline, the P.L. "We certainly wouldn't have been the first Patrol to have its tent gadgeted if we hadn't been able to make our own gadgets."

"And, Shelagh," added Lyn, "you wouldn't have been able to make Q.M. that smashing washing-up table and pot-stand so quickly, or that rope-ladder for us to use a tree as our rest-hour den."

Shelagh was the newest recruit. She had been so keen to get to camp that she had her rucksack packed about a fortnight before the actual camp. She couldn't wait to get there and could not understand why anyone should have to learn things about camping beforehand.

"Okay! I'll admit knowing knots certainly helps you make a gadget, especially one that stands, and helps you tie your bedroll securely," agreed Shelagh.

Peta, another of the Forget-Me-Not Patrol, deftly finished off her well-wrapped bedding. "But," she asked, "what about that rope-ladder nonsense? I doubt if we'll use that for anything more useful than climbing that tree—which I can jolly well climb, anyway!"

Peta was really only teasing, because Shelagh was quite thrilled by the idea of climbing a rope-ladder into the tree. She was very enthusiastic and rushed round trying to learn everything and do every duty herself. Both Peta and Lyn were excellent campers and very knowledgeable about all the camping skills.

"Don't say too much," said Lyn. "Camp isn't over. We might need it yet!"

"Come on, you lot!" called Joanne, the Patrol Second, from inside the tent. "Get your bedrolls stacked quickly. Skipper is calling us. It's almost time to change duties—we're cooks next, I think."

"Look, Skipper is talking to a policeman," said Caroline. "I wonder if anything's wrong."

Skipper, as their Guider, Mrs Whiteside, was called at camp, was talking to one of three policemen who had driven onto the campsite.

"I bet he's here to borrow our rope-ladder! Scotland Yard or MI5 must have heard about our secret weapon, and they want it," laughed Lyn.

"If you don't stop going on about our rope-ladder we'll duck you in the river, and that's a promise," Joanne threatened.

The campsite was situated in the grounds of a large country estate, but far enough away from the manor-house for the Guides to be completely private. The grounds were beautiful, and there was a river winding through the woods and fields.

"Guides, can you all come here for a moment, please? I would like to have a few words with you before you go off to do your new duties." Skipper called them around her as the police-car drove off. "You probably all saw me talking to a police-officer just now. He called to see if we could help him."

They were startled by the sudden appearance of a short, thick-set, bearded man

"What did I tell you?" hissed Lyn under her breath.

"Shut up, Lyn!" Caroline hissed back.

"It appears," Skipper continued, "that a burglary took place in the big house. Some very rare gold coins were taken. They were in a steel box, which has gone. The police have no clue to the thief, and the coins have not been discovered. The police think the coins have not yet been smuggled out of the country and even that they could be hidden somewhere in these grounds. They would appreciate our help. During your hikes and Patrol outings will you be especially observant?"

Discussing the matter later the Guides agreed it would be lovely if they could find the missing coins. It would be a nice way to say thank-you to Major and Mrs Scott for letting Guides use part of their grounds for camping each year.

When the excitement died down the important matter of arranging their big party took precedence over all else. Peta and Denise, the "terrible twins" of the Forget-Me-Not Patrol, were celebrating their first camp and their eleventh birthday all in one, so Skipper and the Patrol Leaders had decided a party was called for.

At the Patrol Leaders' Council it was agreed that each Patrol should make something special in the way of "eats" for the party. Q.M. answered the call by producing block chocolate, rice krispies, tins of fruit, fancy biscuits, instant whips, and a variety of other delicacies.

The Forget-Me-Not Patrol decided to make jellies to go with their tins of fruit. Q.M. warned them to measure the water used carefully or they would have jelly-water, as they had yesterday when the Orchid Patrol were cooks. As it was very warm weather and they had no fridge, they had to give the jellies as much time as possible to set and to find a cool place to keep them.

Very carefully the Guides mixed the jellies, one red and one green, in two borrowed aluminium basins.

"They should be fine once they set," said Joanne, as she licked her wooden spoon.

"I know they will be," agreed Peta, "but will they set? It's very warm. We must find a really cool place for them."

"I know! Let's put them in the river." Lyn lifted one of the basins as she spoke and put a muslim cover over it. "Nothing could be much cooler than that river—it's always freezing."

The local Scouts had roped off part of the river near the site and made it suitable and safe for swimming, but the water was always very cold.

"That's a good idea," agreed Denise. "I agree with Lyn."

So the two jellies were ceremoniously carried to the river and jammed firmly between two rocks at the edge. Skipper had suggested that the Guides might like to spend the morning in the village, so that they could get a few extra things for the party that evening.

As the girls set off, they were startled by the sudden appearance of a short, thick-set, bearded man, who gave them a swift glance and then hurried away in the opposite direction.

"I say, he gave me quite a start!" exclaimed Peta. "Where did he spring from?"

"'Spring' is the right word," said Lyn, rather grimly. "He sprang up from behind that bush. I believe he'd been watching us put our jellies in the river."

"I only hope he won't sneak 'em, that's all," said Shelagh.

"Not till they're set, anyway!" laughed Lyn.

They soon forgot about the bearded man, and hurried on to the village.

On their return to camp they were tired and hungry and ready for the stew they had been promised. After their meal and rest they would be ready to start preparing for the party.

"Now, aren't you all glad I insisted we took the time to prepare the stew and put it into the haybox before we left?" Pat, the Q.M., asked. "Just think how you would all feel if we had to start from scratch and cook our lunch now."

"I just couldn't have made it," gasped Claire, one of the Bluebell Patrol, jokingly.

"I do wish you would all shut up and get the sitters out and the table set; the stew is ready but the orderlies are not," said Denise, as she emerged from the store-tent with a tray full of salt and pepper pots, milk jugs, etc.

Suddenly there was a shout from the river. Lyn had decided to go down to see how the jellies were coming on. "One of the jellies has gone!" she shouted, as she waved from the river-bank.

"What did I tell you?" cried Shelagh. "That bearded man's snatched it! He saw us put the jellies in the river and as soon as we were out of sight he stole 'em."

"He only took one," Joanne pointed out. "Perhaps the other was too runny!"

"Joanne, will you go down and check? You know what Lyn is like. She's probably pulling our legs," said Caroline, and took the loaded tray from Denise.

"Lyn, do stop fooling," Joanne called as she and Denise ran down to join Lyn at the river-bank.

"I'm not fooling. I wish I were. When I got there there was no sign of the second jelly, and it would be the red one that has gone," moaned Lyn.

"Never mind which blinking one is missing; just remember the basin Skipper let us have is only hired by us; it belongs to the County equipment."

"Gosh, Joanne, you're right! I hadn't thought of that."

As none of the other Patrols had hidden it for a joke or knew anything about it, it seemed as if the bearded man had taken it or it had simply floated off. After a hasty meal a general search took place along the river-bank. The Forget-Me-Nots couldn't bear to lose their red jelly. After all, it was their contribution to the party. None of them really believed the bearded man had taken it.

Lyn, Peta and Shelagh decided to go on directly to the old bridge that spanned the river and marked the boundary of the estate. Beyond was out of bounds to the Guides. Lyn remembered noticing how all the old pieces of wood, branches and twigs that fell into the river somewhere along its route seemed to congregate under and around the pillars of the bridge. There might be just a chance that the basin had got trapped between this dead wood.

When they reached the bridge there was no sign of any basin on their side, and they couldn't follow the river as it disappeared into the shade under the bridge. To see the other side of the river and check whether the basin was there, they would have to leave their field and climb over the fence and on to the roadway of

which the bridge formed part. They knew that was out of bounds to them, but a "small look" wouldn't do any harm, Lyn told the other two Guides.

They looked over the farthest wall of the bridge. Sure enough, there was the basin, complete with muslin cover, lodged between some fallen branches! This part of the river was private property, as a *No Trespassing* sign told them, so they could not get down to the river-bank without trespassing, and they didn't have the time to go looking for the owner's house to ask permission. The river was too deep to wade out to the jelly; the only way to reach it was to climb down the centre pillar of the bridge. The river on that side of the bridge was very different from the clear sparkling river that flowed through the campsite. Here it was dark and rather menacing, with the overhanging tree casting strange dancing shadows on the surface, the sun hardly penetrating at all.

"I'll run back to camp and get our rope-ladder," shouted Lyn to Peta and Shelagh. She was already halfway back across the road and over the fence before they could reply. "You two stay

She could stretch out towards the basin

there and watch that the basin doesn't take off again. If it does, follow it and leave me a sign; I'll come after you."

"We can't follow it, Lyn. That part of the river is out of bounds. We shouldn't even be up here on the bridge," Shelagh called after her, but Lyn either didn't hear or ignored the call.

The basin was still in the same spot when Lyn, panting from her exertions and carrying the rope-ladder, ran back to join them.

"Thank goodness you're back!" cried Shelagh. "If I look at that basin much longer I'll develop crossed eyes."

"Me too," added Peta. "It was just beginning to move, unless it was my imagination. Anyway, let's try to get it from here. I don't fancy the look of those woods on this side, apart from their being out of bounds."

"Not to worry! We'll soon have it up." Lyn unrolled the rope-ladder. "I think Shelagh had better go down; she's lighter than either of us."

"I don't mind, but who's going to hold it while I climb down?" asked Shelagh.

"We will, of course, silly!" Lyn threw the end of the rope-ladder down the side of the bridge towards the water.

"Gosh, Lyn, do you think I'll be safe? The river looks very deep from here, and I can't see the bottom!"

"It isn't too deep. It's dark because of the overhanging trees. Get a move on! Peta and I will hold the rope-ladder firmly. We'll wind it round ourselves."

"I'm not a good swimmer," muttered Shelagh.

Cautiously, she climbed on to the top of the bridge and then very slowly down the rungs of the rope-ladder towards the water. By holding on to the ladder with one hand and balancing one foot on a log, she could stretch out towards the basin. After a few unsuccessful attempts she was at last able to draw it towards her and then lift it out of the water and rest it on one of the rungs.

"I've got it!" she yelled. "Hurry up and pass down the bag. I'll put the basin in it so that you can pull it up."

"For goodness' sake, Shelagh, don't get so excited! You'll drop the basin back into the river if you aren't careful."

"Besides," Peta added, "every time you dance about it is harder to hold you."

Perhaps it was the excitement of saving the jelly, or she may have just lost her footing, or the branch may have floated off, but as the jelly was safely on its way up in the string bag, down into the river went Shelagh! The water was deep enough for her to go under, but she kept hold of the bottom rung of the ladder and so was able to keep her head above the water.

"Oh, Shelagh, hang on! Don't let go, for goodness' sake!" called Lyn. "We'll see if we can pull you up."

It was very different holding the rope-ladder steady while Shelagh climbed carefully down it from trying to pull it up with her hanging on to it. The two couldn't do it; they could just about manage to hold Shelagh so that her head stayed above the water.

"Don't panic, Shelagh!" cried Lyn. "Listen! If we hold the ladder steady could you climb up? We can't pull you up by ourselves."

But all Shelagh could do was to hold on. Neither Lyn nor Peta could let go her end of the rope and run for help. One alone couldn't sustain the weight of Shelagh.

"Oh, Lyn," cried Shelagh, trying to keep the sob out of her voice, "I don't think I can hold on for very much longer! My hands and arms are getting cramped and I'm very cold."

"Can you feel around with your feet and see if you can find a large stone or anything that you could get your feet on to take the strain off your arms and so that you can keep your head above water?" Lyn said desperately.

"I'll try," answered Shelagh, who was now shivering with

Shelagh managed to scramble on to what she took to be a large rock or an old tree-trunk

cold, "but it's not very easy."

The Guides on the bridge tightened their hold on the rope-ladder as Shelagh felt around under the water with her feet. She was about to give up when her leg hit something.

"I think I've found something," she called. "It's almost under the bridge."

"Never mind about where it is," Lyn called back. "If you can get your feet on to it it will take the strain from you."

"Yes, and from us too, I hope," said Peta, who was also feeling the strain.

As Shelagh swung towards the arch of the bridge again, Peta and Lyn tightened their grip on the rope. After one or two tries, Shelagh managed to scramble on to what she took to be a large rock or an old tree-trunk. To have the weight taken off her arms was such a relief that she almost cried.

"Good show!" cried Peta, thankful to have Shelagh's weight taken off Lyn and herself.

As Shelagh got her balance she relaxed a little and began to look around her.

"Lyn," she called, "I don't think this is a rock at all, nor a tree-trunk, either. It seems too square and smooth. It's a kind of box or chest."

She traced the shape of the box tentatively with one foot while trying to keep her balance with the other.

"Take care, Shelagh, for goodness' sake," called Peta. "We don't want you to fall in again. It must be an old tin or something like that."

"It isn't!" Shelagh let out a sudden cry. "It's a box—iron or steel! Lyn, Peta, do you think it could be the stolen coins?"

"Gosh!" cried Lyn. "It could be! It may have been hidden in the river!"

The girls were so excited that they didn't notice a thick-set, bearded man emerge quietly from the belt of trees bordering the river. He climbed the fence.

"Are you in trouble?" he asked. "I heard you calling out."

"No, not really," said Lyn; "that is," she added confusedly, "our friend can't get out of the river. We weren't strong enough to haul her up the rope-ladder, but now she's found—er—something to stand on we can go back to our camp and bring help."

"No need to do that," said the man. "I'm sure I can pull hard enough to get your friend back up. She looks very cold."

"Thank you," said Lyn, who would have preferred to do without the stranger's help, but could hardly refuse it.

It didn't take the girls long, with the substantial help of the bearded man, to bring Shelagh out of the water and on to the bridge.

"Thank you," she said to the bearded man, and the others added their thanks.

The bearded man hesitated. "I couldn't help hearing what the young lady said when she was in the water. She said she thought there was a steel box in the river. Is that what you are searching for?"

"Great Scott, no!" cried Lyn. "We were searching for a jelly."

"A jelly?" queried the bearded man, obviously startled.

The girls laughed. They were feeling more relaxed now; the bearded man seemed much less sinister than they had imagined him at first sight.

"We put two jellies in the river to set," explained Peta, "but when we went to get them out one of them had disappeared. It had floated away. We spotted it from the bridge, and Shelagh climbed down the rope-ladder and fished it up; then she couldn't get back."

"And she found something else, eh?" asked the bearded man quietly.

"I don't know for sure that it is a box," Shelagh told him.

"I have a shrewd idea that it is, and that it may well be the box of coins stolen from Major Scott."

The Guides stared at him. None of them spoke.

"My name is Hawkins," went on the bearded man—"Detective Hawkins, of the Bantrick police. I have been keeping a watch in these grounds and on the river. I suspected that the gold coins were hidden by the thief, who is likely to come back to collect them from wherever they are hidden—most likely at night. When I saw you putting something in the river earlier today, I thought for a moment that you might be hiding the gold coins."

"We're not thieves!" cried Shelagh indignantly.

"I realise that now," Detective Hawkins smiled. "In my job I have to suspect everybody—even Girl Guides."

"Major Scott will be very pleased to hear that the gold coins have been found," said Lyn.

Detective Hawkins shook his head. "I shall not tell him—yet. I hope you won't either. I propose to leave the box where it is and lie in wait for the thief to collect it. I want you to say nothing about your discovery. If the thief got even a hint that the loot had been located he wouldn't come near it. What I want to do is to catch him redhanded with the stolen goods in his possession."

"My name is Hawkins," went on the bearded man—"Detective Hawkins"

"That makes sense," Peta nodded. "We won't say anything, eh, Shelagh?"

"I'll keep mum," Shelagh promised. "I wish we could see the thief captured, though!"

"You can," Detective Hawkins said unexpectedly. "From now on I shall lie in wait with a couple of constables. If you girls care to come along after dusk and promise to keep absolutely quiet, you may be able to take part in the apprehension of the thief. I can't be sure that he will come tonight, but my guess is that he won't wait longer than he thinks is safe to collect the booty."

"We'll say nothing, and we'll sneak away after supper," said Peta, excitedly. "What d'you say, Lyn?"

"I'd love to be in at the death," admitted Lyn.

"It'll be a terrific adventure," chortled Shelagh.

"Good!" said Detective Hawkins. "Not a word till then. I'll see you later—but tread softly! I'm sure your Girl Guide training will enable you to do that."

"You won't hear us coming," promised Peta.

"We must get back to camp to dry Shelagh out now, Mr Hawkins," said Lyn. "Come on, girls."

The girls ran most of the way back to camp. While Shelagh changed into dry clothes, Lyn and Peta sought out Skipper and told her what had happened.

"Shelagh and Peta promised to say nothing about it," explained Lyn, "but I was careful not to make a promise that I might have to break. I believed Mr Hawkins at first, but when he said he'd lie in wait for the thief to collect the box of coins, I became pretty sure that he isn't a detective."

"Whatever made you think he isn't, Lyn?" cried Peta in surprise.

"Because if he was going to keep watch for the thief to pick up the box he'd want to make absolutely sure first that the box Shelagh said she'd touched in the river was the box of stolen coins instead of just accepting that it was without even making a check. *He knew it was the stolen box. He knew because he put it there himself.* My guess is that he's just waiting for a chance to get it out of the river. I believe he'll bring it out without waiting another minute."

"Gosh, yes!" cried Peta. "No wonder he wanted us to keep quiet about it! I'm sure you're right, Lyn."

"It sounds like very sharp thinking on your part, Lyn," said Skipper quietly. "It is my duty to notify the police about what has happened. I'll run over to the police-station at once. I'll soon find out whether there is a Detective Hawkins."

"I hope Mr Detective Hawkins doesn't get away with the coins before Skipper gets back with the police," said Peta when Skipper had gone.

"It's up to us to see that he doesn't," said Lyn. "Let's tell Caroline and the rest of the Patrol. I vote we all go along to the bridge and see that the box of coins stays put till the police arrive—that is, if Mr Hawkins is a fake."

"That's a good idea, Lyn," Caroline, the P.L., said when she heard Lyn's suggestion. "On the principle that there's safety in numbers, the whole Patrol and as many others as we can muster in a hurry will go to the bridge and stay there till Skipper arrives with the police, which shouldn't be long."

Within minutes Caroline and Lyn were leading a dozen eager Guides towards the bridge. On reaching the bridge, Lyn let out a shout. Emerging from the water, clutching a steel box, was Mr Hawkins!

"Just in time!" muttered Peta.

"Hello, Mr Hawkins!" Lyn called out. "You decided not to leave the box in the river for the thief to collect, then?"

Mr Hawkins was nonplussed. He gazed in dismay and anger at the Guides. He spluttered something that the girls didn't catch, but he clearly realised that he was in a situation he couldn't easily talk his way out of. He had little chance of doing so, for the arrival of Skipper shortly afterwards with a plain-clothes detective and two uniformed constables completed his defeat.

"So it was you, Hawkins!" said the detective. "I didn't know you were operating in these parts—as a detective too! Thanks to these smart Girl Guides, we've caught you in time—redhanded with the booty!"

When Hawkins had been taken away, Skipper said, "This will be a really nice thank-you to Major and Mrs Scott for their kindness to us, Guides. Very well done, Lyn and the Forget-Me-Nots!"

All the Guides agreed that the Forget-Me-Nots had made a brilliant contribution to the camp party.

"All I hope now," said Shelagh, "is that you'll all like our jellies too."

"You ought to," added Peta. "One of 'em nearly got away."

Mud Faces

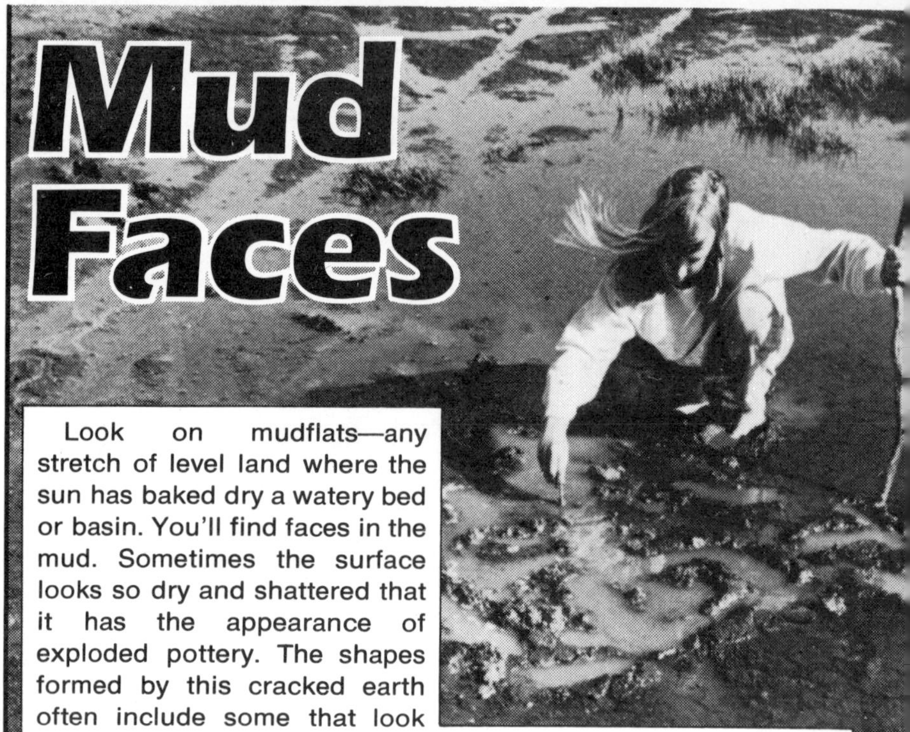

Look on mudflats—any stretch of level land where the sun has baked dry a watery bed or basin. You'll find faces in the mud. Sometimes the surface looks so dry and shattered that it has the appearance of exploded pottery. The shapes formed by this cracked earth often include some that look like human faces—perhaps more like caricatures. Some can look like profiles of people of an ancient civilisation or like the reliefs you see on Grecian urns or Roman friezes.

Faces may be complete just as found. Others will look more lifelike if you add a pebble to make an eye or cut a slit for a mouth. It could help to clarify a face if you remove some of the bits of earth or stones nearby, isolating it to make it stand out clearly.

This isn't an activity you embark on in a newly ironed Guide uniform, but it can be fun, and what's nicer than a patch of clean, well-baked mud?

Mudflat artist *(above, left)*

Head of Roman emperor—or is it Aunt Agatha? *(left)*

Photos by Alan Band Associates

Badge Jackpot

It may surprise you to know there are fourteen badges involved in putting on a winter concert.

Dramatic sketches, 6-10 minutes in length, are needed for the Challenge and Writer badges. Allow approximately 130 words per minute, less if there's plenty of action. Keep the dialogue short and crisp. Open the show with a light-hearted item; comedy always appeals to an audience. End with a short one-act play, serious or not, followed by a rousing Campfire.

Choose lively solo and chorus items for the Dancer, Country Dancer, Musician, Folk Singer, Speaker and Entertainer badges. For a first venture keep the programme simple but varied. Mix the dances, songs and sketches for a well-balanced show. Resist the tendency to gabble the words. Try the old stage trick of a few deep breaths to help you relax first. Aim your voice at the back of the hall and check with the producer that it reaches there! Rehearse on stage and in costume as often as possible.

Always get permission to use stage facilities. If doing your own make-up use the special Leichner face-charts as a guide. However, older people might be willing to do both the stage lighting and make-up for you.

Costume-making covers all clauses for Needlewoman. Draw sketches of each character's dress, putting each one when made into a labelled plastic bag. Use bright, harmonizing colours that will not fade into the scenery. Haunt your local jumble sales for suitable clothing and material. Old curtains are excellent for cloaks, togas, saris and crinolines. Gold and silver paint sprays can transform shoes or dull materials. Crêpe paper is invaluable for frills, lengthening dresses, overskirts, fringes, or added to a basic outfit of tights and leotard.

Invite old people, or Brownies perhaps, to your final dress-rehearsal as this will give you valuable experience in playing before an audience. Take interior, portrait and action shots for part of the Photographer badge. Sell these photos at the actual concert, or at your next Open Evening.

Clause 1 of the Artist badge could be met by including a scene appropriate to the background of the concert. Use a large brush and thick poster-paints. Boots and other shops sell inexpensive containers of these. Working from a small-scale drawing, roughly sketch in an outline on the scenery paper with charcoal. Often newsprinters will sell "end rolls" of paper cheap—try contacting your local newspaper office. Pin the paper to a light-weight wooden frame made for the Carpenter badge.

Serve refreshments during the interval for the Hostess badge. The following is a guide to catering for a hundred people: Have two 12-16 pint teapots and allow one teaspoonful of tea per pint. You will need 4 pints of milk, ½lb of tea, 2lbs of sugar and 4 packets of sweet biscuits. Serve the sugar in bowls, the biscuits on plates, and charge 5p per cup of tea with biscuit.

The Flower Arranger can decorate the refreshment-table with posies. She can also, as given in clause 1, create a "mass" effect in large containers for either side of the stage.

It can be great fun working for these badges in the exciting atmosphere of a concert. Finally, don't forget to invite the various badge-testers to the show!

Make a Patrol Tapestry

Lena Baker Explains How

A Patrol "tapestry" need not be expensive if you can obtain a plastic-type vegetable bag from the local market or from a greengrocer. These bags are usually discarded after use, so should cost you nothing. When opened up, the bag is just like a length of tapestry. Being an oblong shape, it enables two or more Guides to work on it at the same time.

Materials Required: Gather together as many balls of odd wool as possible—perhaps wool left over after garments have been knitted. The more colours you can include the better. You will also need blunt bodkins, chalk, a little thick poster-paint—black if possible, although any colour will do—and one large plastic-type woven bag, the kind used to contain carrots, onions or, sometimes, fruit at the greengrocer's. These bags are usually thrown away after being emptied; the family greengrocer would probably give you one.

Now carefully unpick the stitching around your plastic-type bag, which will then resemble a length of tapestry. Stretch it out into an oblong shape. The edges on this type of bag are non-run, so you will have no need to sew any hems.

Decide on a design. A woodland, camping or seashore scene might be chosen, or you might prefer your Patrol emblem or flags of different countries.

If you have an artist in your Patrol, she could draw your design directly on to the tapestry in chalk. If no one in the Patrol is good at freehand drawing, draw the design on to paper first. When satisfied with it, cut it out and lay it on to your tapestry as a pattern and draw around it in chalk.

If you judge your chalk outline to be good enough, paint over in poster-paint, allowing it to dry overnight.

With your wool and bodkins, fill in the design drawn, using suitable stitches. Some stitches suitable are illustrated.

When you have filled in the design on your tapestry, complete by filling in all the background around in one colour, or, if an outdoor scene, make the top half blue to represent sky and the bottom half green to represent grass.

You can now fix the tapestry to the wall of your Patrol corner, though you may like to frame it first.

Stitches suitable for Patrol tapestry

Caught under netting at these points

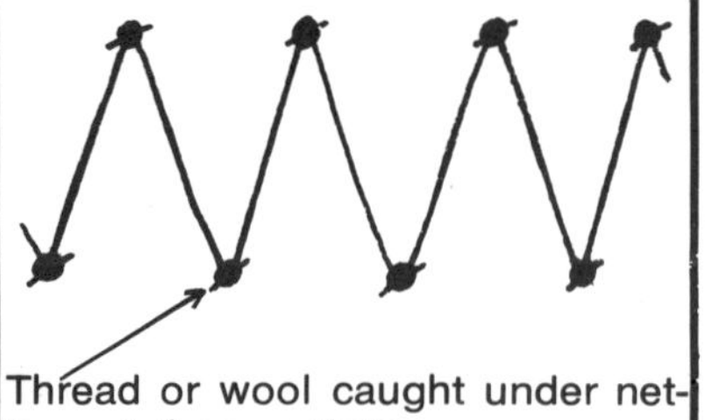

Thread or wool caught under netting at these points.

Caught under netting

Running-stitch in and out of netting; weave, passing your thread under on one row and over net on next row, rather as bricks are laid

Thread or wool passes behind netting here

Make a Garden Kneeler

M. I. Eckhardt Shows You How

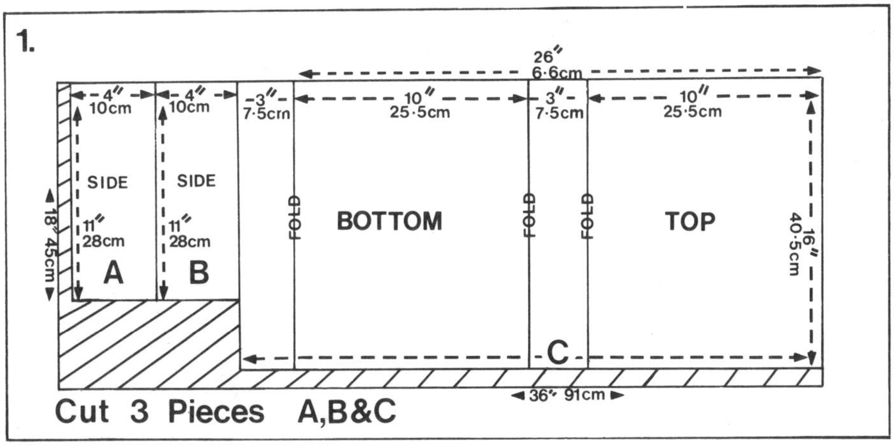

Materials needed

Foam, size 40.5×25.5 cm (16×10 ins) and 7.5 cm (3 ins) thick
Plastic bag
45.5 cm (½ yd) of 91.5 cm (36 ins)-wide material to cover
Press studs

To make

1. Cut out material as shown.
2. Sew on the side pieces with a backstitch or by machine.
3. Cover foam with plastic bag. Sellotape edge down; this will protect the foam from damp.
4. Fit the foam into its cover.
5. Sew press-studs along open edge to complete.

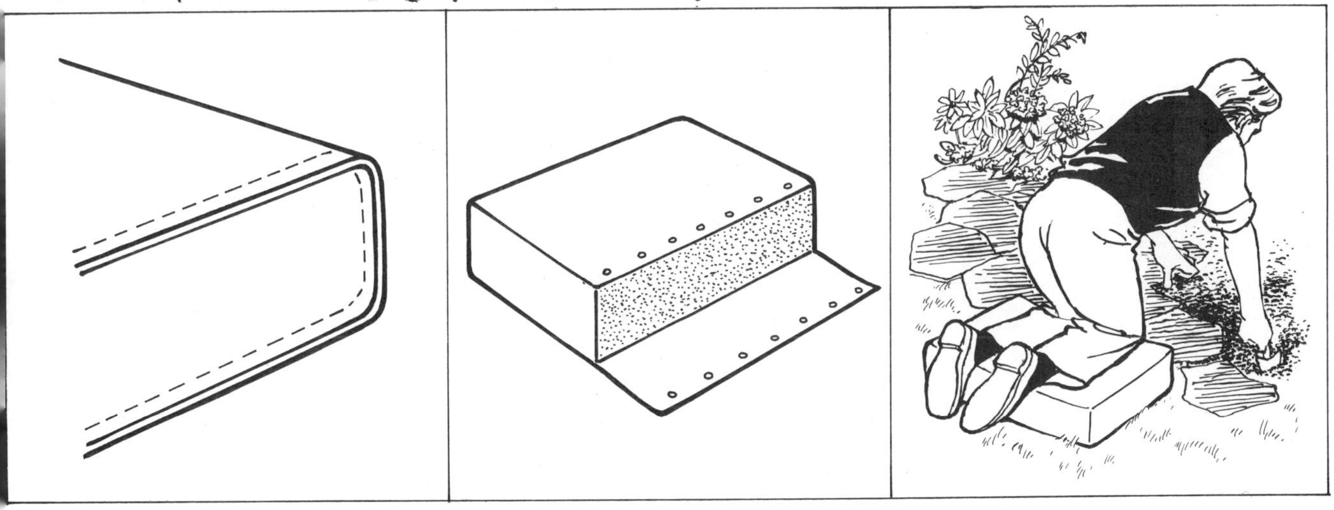

Guides in

Where They Feasted on Whalemeat, Reindeer and Guillemot

by Jean Williams

An exciting exchange of visits between Guides of the 1st Failand Company, Bristol, and Guides of Copenhagen, Denmark, began in 1971 and has continued ever since.

During a camp to celebrate the 250th anniversary of the founding of modern Greenland, the Bristol Guides went on an unforgettable hike that included walking on sand in the unusual temperature of 26.7° C or 80° F to see the inland ice-cap, camping near Holsteinsborg, and feasting on whalemeat, reindeer, cod, and guillemot.

Back home, the Failand Guides corresponded with the Hans Egede Troop of Copenhagen, and the 1st Failand Brownies did the same with the Hans Egede Brownie Pack. Later, the Guides travelled to Denmark and spent a wonderful two weeks with their Danish friends, camping in Central Jutland and sightseeing in Copenhagen, covering what seemed to be the whole of that city in one afternoon! On the final evening the Bristol Guides entertained with national songs and dances.

The Danes returned the visit the following year, camping in Britain, visiting famous beauty-spots, and ending with a day in London and a night at Olave House.

Friendship continued, and thirty-three of us lived together in a chalet five hundred feet above Grindelwald, at Muhlebach, in Switzerland. We shopped and cooked for ourselves and spent most of our days walking. We visited the glaciers and the glacier gorge, climbed to the Swiss Alpine Club hut (the Glecksteinhutte), on the Wetterhorn, glided silently over the tree-tops on the longest chair-lift in Europe to the terminus of First, and visited "Our Chalet", at Adelboden.

The time to say goodbye came all too soon, but our wonderful exchange visits go on, illustrating the true family spirit of Guiding.

Above
Holsteinsborg, Greenland, in its setting of rugged mountains

Inset, right
A long climb up ladders to the Upper Glacier above Grindelwald, Switzerland

Right
The ice-cap, Greenland

Denmark

Beat the Bounds

P. Thompson Suggests an Expedition for Explorer Pennant

What will you need if you plan to beat the parish bounds? The most useful things will be a large-scale map, a stout pair of shoes, and enough refreshments for a long day out.

Nowadays the divisions between parishes are clearly marked by the recognised symbol on Ordnance Survey maps, available for all districts. But this has not always been the case, and the information about such boundary-marks then had to be passed from one generation to another.

This was the origin of the custom of proceeding around the parish once a year, usually at Rogation-tide, which precedes Ascension Day. Sometimes this was called Cross Week, as crosses were carried in the procession, or Grass Week, because Rogation days were fast days and the food was mainly vegetarian.

The ceremony took place in towns as well as villages; it still survives in some places. The clergy and local officials led the way, and accompanying them went a crowd of boys, who generally carried twigs, often of willow.

The actual beating of the boundary-stones and other marks was an important part of the custom; but in some cases it was the boys themselves who were bumped on the stones and on other landmarks such as walls, gates and trees. This made it even more likely that they would remember them well! No doubt they were cheered by the thought of the refreshments that usually followed the walk.

Prayers for a blessing on the crops might be said, or a psalm sung, or a lesson read from the Bible, at certain stopping-places. The name of "Gospel Oak" or "Gospel Ash", occasionally seen on a map, recalls this.

The custom fulfilled a very useful purpose, and when it tended to die out in the seventeenth century many disputes about land ownership followed. Sometimes the stones were moved by unscrupulous people in order to acquire more ground. There is an old rhyme emphasising this:

> That ev'ry man might keepe his owne possessions,
> Our forefathers us'd, in reverent processions
> (With zealous prayers and with praiseful cheere),
> To walke their parish limits once a yeare,
> And well known markes (which sacrilegious handes
> Now cut or breake) so bordered out their landes,
> That every one distinctly knew his owne,
> And many brawles, now rife, were then unknowne.

Over the years the land has often been put to different uses, and where the beating of the bounds still continues or has been revived there may be difficulties to surmount. For instance, at Crompton, in Lancashire, it is now necessary to swim across a reservoir and crawl through an outlet tunnel if the perambulation is to be complete!

There are other places where boundary-stones are in or near rivers. In the parish of St. Clement Dane, London, a choirboy has to be held by the heels as he reaches to touch a mark beside the River Thames in the Temple Gardens. At Richmond, Yorkshire, there is a stone in the middle of the River Swale. A boat used to be taken out to touch this, but one year it capsized, so now people wade out or stones are thrown at the mark.

The ceremony at the Tower of London is held every three years and has not changed since 1555. The choristers strike at the thirty-one boundary-marks with white wands, while the Chief Warder commands, "Whack it, boys, whack it!" And at each stone the Chaplain calls out, "Cursed is he who removeth his neighbour's landmark."

You may be lucky enough to find some of these boundary-stones still in place. In the north part of Kensington Gardens, in

# of a Parish

Photo by Alan Band Associates

Choirgirls and choirboys thoroughly enjoy beating the bounds of the Tower of London, a custom carried on for hundreds of years

London, there are several. They mark the boundary of the former Paddington Parish and the old Metropolitan Borough of Paddington, and have the initials "P.P." or "M.B.P." on them.

In contrast, there is the Edgarley Stone beside the road in a lonely spot between Simonsbath and Challacombe, on the line of the old Exmoor Forest boundary, on the Somerset-Devon border.

On some of the old six-inch-to-the-mile maps, the stones are shown; perhaps a local farmer or landowner has a copy. It is a good plan to ask the Vicar or someone who knows the district well to help you plan the expedition. You will need to know the owners of any fields that you must cross in the country parish so that you can ask permission beforehand. This is most readily given at a time of year when the corn or grass is not high and you will not damage crops.

Remember to work out how long the walk will be. It may be too long to do all in one day. In 1900 it took three days to "Bump the Bounds" of the City of Bristol. All the officials, together with three hundred policemen as well as trumpeters and banner-bearers, went along. You are likely to carry out your expedition a little less noisily!

Colour print by Mrs K. P. Morey

Girl Scouts of Ueda, Japan, arrive at their camp-site wearing sweaters and long trousers as a concession to very cold weather but retaining their uniform neck-scarf and hat

East and West

Colour print by Mrs P. E. Robinson

The Guide Family Robinson of England (15th Chelmsford Trinity Methodist Company, Essex), consisting of Patrol Leaders Carol and Susan, Linda, and Brownie Guide Hazel

Three new Queen's Guides of the 6th Beeston (St. Mary's) Company proudly display well-earned certificates

Colour print by Miss S. J. Owen

Pearlies and Wombles join with Guides in fun and games at Putney

Colour prints by Mrs J. Keenan

Great Occasions

Colour print by Mrs Pamela Wood

Colour print depicting 2nd Ramsey Guides by Mrs H. Pye

"Come into my parlour," the Mayor of Ealing invites Guides of the 13th Ealing (St. Stephen's) Company, who see the civic regalia in company with their Guider—the Mayoress

These busy Guides ironing, cooking, shoe-cleaning, gardening, and looking after babies are demonstrating their theme of helping others as their float rolls along in the local carnival at Ramsey, Isle of Man

Are You a Water Diviner?

Get Your Patrol to Try Their Hand with a Hazel Twig

A water-diviner at work

Photo by Alan Band Associates

Suggests Alan Major

One of the methods used in the past to find water was with a divining rod. This consisted of a forked piece of a hazel branch formed in a Y or V shape and about 30cm (12″) long. Try it! One end of the fork is held in each closed hand with the knuckles upwards or downwards, depending on which is the most comfortable, while the joined end of the twig points away from the body and is kept level with the ground. The "diviner" then walks slowly round or across the area where there may be water. If water is there the twig moves and seems to come alive, dipping and jerking downwards.

Some diviners use rods made of brass, steel, ivory or whalebone in the form of an L shape, the bottom part of the L being held in the hand while the longer part points in front. One rod is held in each hand, and as the user draws closer to water the two rods meet and cross each other, forming a cross in front of the user and over the site of the water.

To try to find water, cut a piece of hazel twig of the shape described. If hazel is not available, blackthorn is quite suitable. You could bury a tin of water in a square of meadow or other space and invite your Patrol to "divine" it.

You may get a surprise! You may find something else besides water! Using either a rod or a twig, diviners are sometimes employed to find missing cables, underground pipes, drains, buried manhole covers, building foundations, and even coins and missing objects. Perhaps you would like to try for hidden "treasure" of this kind. Instead of a tin of water, bury only the empty tin ten to twenty centimetres (4″×8″) below the surface, then get your Patrol members to see if the twig or rod jerks downwards or moves into a cross as the hidden tin is reached.

No one knows who first tried water-divining in Britain, but the hazel-twig is known to have been used in the sixteenth century. Diviners were considered important people. Sometimes the failure or success of a crop depended on their being able to find water. Many worked with well-diggers and could say exactly how deep the water was situated.

How does divining work? One belief is that every object gives off radiations which the diviner receives through the twig or rod. Another is that the diviner himself gives off radiations, like radar, which strike the unseen water or object and are then picked up through the rod or twig. Another theory is that diviners have extra-sensory perception, the ability to "receive" radiations through a kind of sixth sense.

Even if you don't find water or buried treasure your Patrol members will enjoy testing their powers.

HAVE FUN With Cakes

For the Hostess Badge

by Brenda Morton

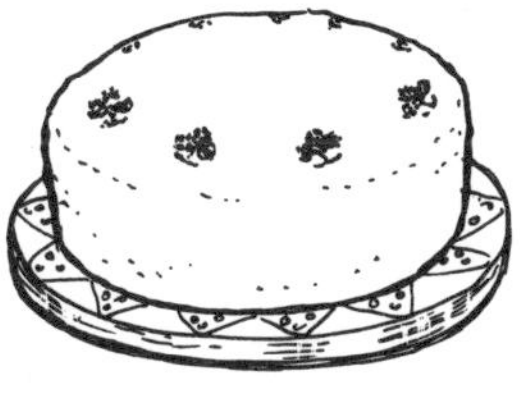

Cake Motifs

Make coloured-sugar decorations. Draw Guide motif on square of clean card. Cut out motif, leaving card with shaped hole. Place card over cake. Brush through hole with a little milk. Sprinkle on coloured sugar. Remove card carefully, leaving coloured motif.

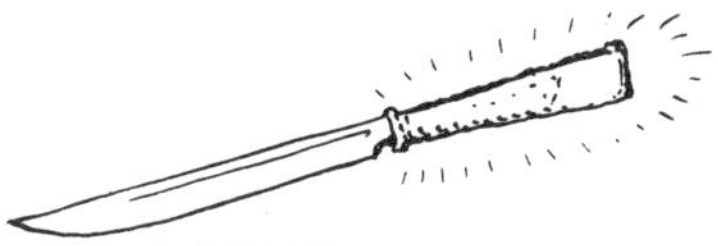

Ceremonial Knife

Cut the cake at a party with a large and magnificent silver knife. Merely use a carving knife, having covered the handle with silver paper!

Cake Frills

Cake need only be iced on top. Cut strips of crepe paper. Fringe top and bottom. Sew greaseproof paper along back. Paste cut-out Guide motifs on front.

Coloured Sugar

Make coloured sugar for decorating cakes by putting castor sugar in a screwtop jar. Add a few drops of vegetable colouring. Shake well, and sugar will become coloured. Sprinkle on to iced cake.

SAVE!

SAVE SOAP!

A Thrifty Hint by I. P. Bool

What happens to the small pieces of soap that are left in the bathroom? Collect them and save them until you have enough to fill a small foam bag about 10 cm (4″) square.

Follow the instructions below and see how simple it is.

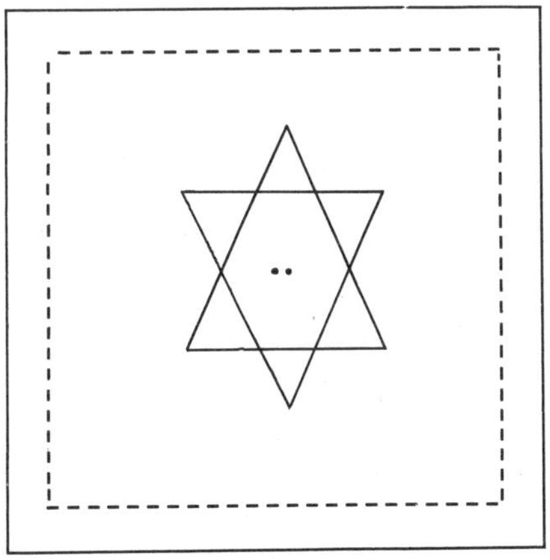

1. Cut two pieces of foam 10cm×10cm.
2. Cut two triangular shapes in another colour.
3. Stitch the two triangular pieces to centre of one piece of foam.
4. Place both pieces together and stitch down three sides.
5. Fill the bag with the soap pieces and stitch up the fourth side.

SAVE LIGHT!

It's more economical to leave the electric light on than to switch it on and off if you're in and out of a room at frequent intervals. More electricity is used when a light is switched on than when left burning for some time. Tell Dad!

SAVE HEAT!

Save electricity or gas by boiling only the quantity of liquid you need rather than filling saucepan or kettle full.

SAVE BOOTS!

Roll up your *TV Times* and *Radio Times* and Mum's glossy magazines after use and put them in your wellies, which will then keep their shape when left standing.

Arts an

Colour print by Mrs C. Jones

In a programme of song and dance to celebrate their fiftieth birthday the 57th Nottingham Guides pose in a scene reminiscent of "The Boy Friend"

Your comments, please, on the performance of the 1st Brampton Guides competing as the Shirley Bassey Dancers in a "New Faces" Christmas entertainment

"How!" The Red Indians, painted and feathered, are quite harmless. They're Guides of the 1st Cranleigh Company at camp

Colour print by Mrs J. Shannon

Crafts

Colour print by Mrs J. Simpson

Colour print by Mrs E. Whitemore

The craft of lacemaking is demonstrated by two Guides from the 1st Hythe (Southampton) Company at a hobbies-and-handicrafts exhibition

Guides of the future will look proudly at this tree and recall that it was planted by Guides of their own Company, the 1st Heath and Reach, Bedfordshire

Colour print by Mrs J. August

Comfort in Camp

by Trevor Holloway

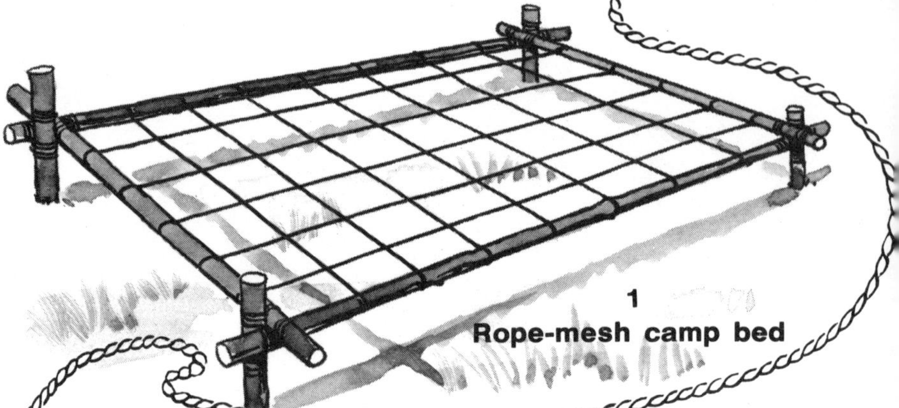

1
Rope-mesh camp bed

Camping is what you make it. You can be as comfortable as the proverbial bug in a rug—or just the reverse. With a little time and ingenuity, plus a few odds and ends such as sticks and string, you can make your camp a home from home—almost, anyway!

You may not be able to afford the luxury of a camp-bed, but that's no reason why you should suffer in wakeful silence whilst the other Guides are snoring their heads off! The de-luxe model illustrated by Fig. 1 can be yours for nothing if you begin collecting odd lengths of rope right away. Your local newsagent may be able to help, as he gets lots of rope from his parcels of daily papers.

The four corner-posts should be about 61 cm (2 ft.) long. Drive them about 23 cm (9 ins.) into the ground. The two side poles should be about 198 cm (6 ft. 6 ins.) and the cross-bars 91 cm (3 ft.).

Lash the four poles securely to the uprights and then tie the ropes in place, keeping them as taut as possible. If you can make use of some ready-made netting—perhaps garden netting or an old hammock—so much the better. Lay a straw palliasse over the netting and you'll have a super job.

Seating is often a problem in camp—*comfortable* seating, that is. A log or an upturned box is a common item of camp furniture, but if you want real comfort how about the "deckchair" seen in Fig. 2? An old sack or piece of canvas and three poles plus some string are all you need. The only snag about this masterpiece is that if you vacate it for a moment someone else bags it!

A frustrating little problem besetting campers is where to hang the mirror. If you lay your mirror on the sloping tent roof, the angle is wrong. If you hang it from a branch it takes great glee in spinning round and round. End your troubles once and for all with the patented

2
Deck-chair

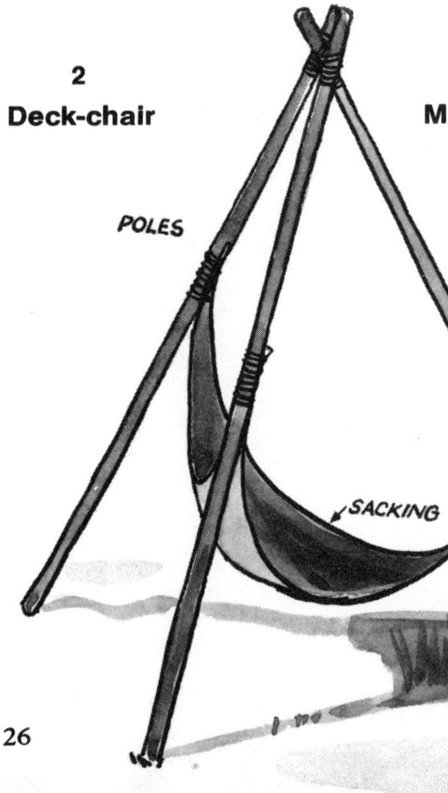

3
Mirror holder

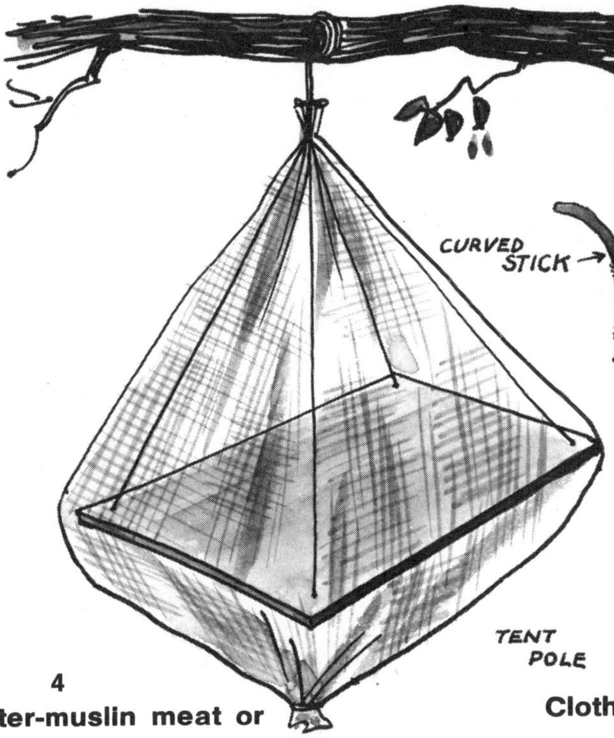

4
Butter-muslin meat or food safe

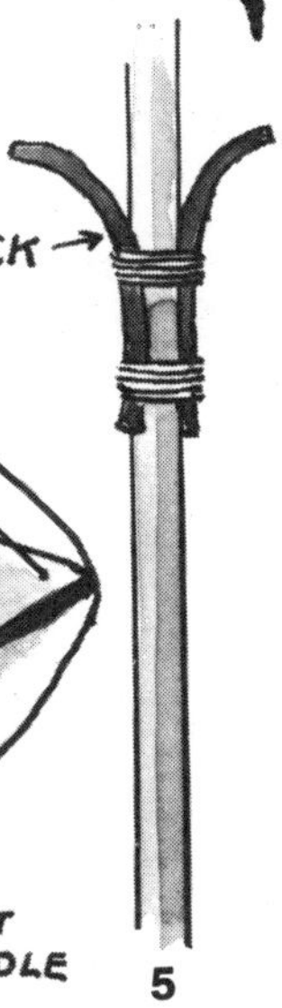

5
Clothes pegs

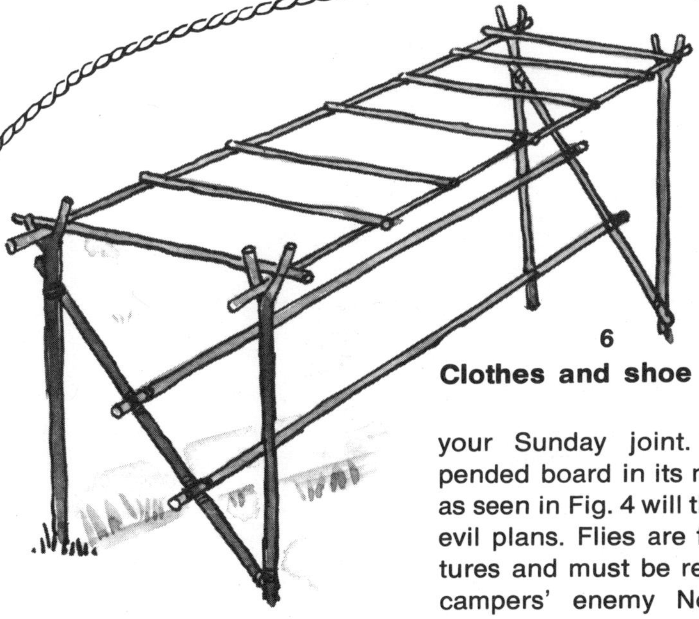

6
Clothes and shoe rack

7
Instant shower

forked stick support advertised in Fig. 3. It is portable and you can lean it at any angle you like. Install one outside your tent and your Patrol will at long last acquire that well-groomed appearance so often lacking except on Visitors' Day!

From mirrors we pass to meat safes. Flies turn up in even the best-run camps, taking a special delight in tracking down your Sunday joint. The suspended board in its muslin bag as seen in Fig. 4 will thwart their evil plans. Flies are filthy creatures and must be regarded as campers' enemy No. 1. You can't have too much butter-muslin in camp, and all the unwrapped foodstuffs should be covered.

A "tidy" idea is to tie some suitably shaped pieces of stick to the tent pole on which to hang hats and coats (Fig. 5). It's surprising how much tidier a tent can be kept if things are hung up instead of being "hung" on the ground for everyone to trample over. Raincoats are too expensive these days to be used as doormats!

The ground is no place for clothes or shoes—even in camp. Better make the combined clothes and shoe rack seen in Fig. 6. By day it can be used as a table for keeping your various possessions neat and tidy.

Can you think of anything more refreshing on a hot day than a cold shower—always supposing you get a hot day at camp, which, of course, is by no means certain, our climate being what it is? Consult Fig. 7 for a gadget that will effectively cool the heated brow—and other parts of your anatomy. Just pull on the rope and treat yourself to a two-gallon shower whenever you feel like it. There's only one rule—leave a full can of water for the next girl.

Time for Fun

Colour print by Miss S. Rackley

'Blind Man's Buff" provides mirth and merriment at Coddeston Campsite, Berkshire, for the 8th Maidenhead (All Saints') Guides

Colour print by Mrs L. J. Field

"I'll blow it and fan it till it does go!" vows this determined camper and cook from the 3rd Headstone Company, Harrow

And baby came too—and thoroughly enjoyed camp life and being fussed over by the Guides of Mum's Company, the 2nd Allington (St. Nicholas'), Kent

Colour print by Mrs C. Jones

Two nosy parkers play the matchstick game at the Lewsey Farm Company's birthday party

Colour print by Miss S. Greenup

Models and Gadgets

Patrol Leaders from Leeds, South-West Division, explore the arts in a variety of creative activities at a training session near Harrogate

Colour slide by Miss S. J. Owen

Knotty problems for these Guides of the 1st Tunbridge Wells (St. Luke's) Company, who are learning to square-lash on a washing-up gadget at camp

Colour slide by Miss Daphne M. Pilcher

The ELEVENTH Guide Law

by Sheila Deft

As Guides, you're often in demand
When trouble looms in view.
But though you're quick to lend a hand
Make certain that you understand
What's needed. Pause a moment and
Consider what to do;
Before you rush with fervent dedication,
Just wait till you've assessed the situation.

If you are on a country hike
And see upon the ground
A figure lying comatose,
Unmoving and with eyelids closed,
Before you start on "mouth-to-nose"
To try to bring him round
Make certain that he really needs your aid—
He may be merely sleeping in the shade!

Or if, with heavy shopping load,
A lady you should meet
As she stands patient by the road,
Don't rush to use your Green Cross Code
And swiftly see her safe-bestowed
Across the busy street.
Make certain first that's where she wants to go—
She may be waiting for a bus, you know!

You're keen to do your daily deed
With modest competence,
But those most likely to succeed
Have more than kindness, skill, and speed—

There is another thing you need
And that is commonsense!
The Founder gave us an eleventh rule—
"Remember that a Guide is not a fool!"

Ghosts and Guides at Chingle Hall

by Michael Edwards

Guider Miss Margaret Smith and Guides take a look at the outside of Chingle Hall

Guides take notes and photographs for their log-book

Twelve Guides from the 39th Preston (Fulwood Methodist) Company paid a visit to Chingle Hall, in the heart of the Lancashire countryside. This strange old house, situated at the end of a long, winding country lane, and surrounded by trees, has the reputation of being haunted. The Guides didn't meet any ghosts, but they heard some eerie stories of them—of ghostly footsteps, unexplained tappings, and spectral apparitions. Well, in a setting like this, with the wind whistling in the trees and the rain lashing against the windows, ghosts can seem very real!

Chingle Hall was used as a centre for secret mass in the days when Roman Catholics were put to death in England for taking part. John Wall, a noted Franciscan monk who was put to death for his faith, was born here in 1620, leaving at the age of eighteen to train for the priesthood.

The Guides' tour began in the chapel, where in 1960 an altar and a pre-Reformation cross were uncovered behind plaster

Mrs Howarth tells Guides how the model galleon "sailed" across the room

The cupboard is really a secret hiding-place in the wall

and rubble. Here they saw a hole in the flagged floor that was used to conceal vessels used in the mass, and, above it, a secret hiding-place or priest-hole, in which the priest conducting the service could hide if an alarm was raised.

The dining-room is the room most favoured for manifestations by the ghosts of Chingle Hall. The owner, Mrs Margaret Howarth, told the Guides that candlesticks have inexplicably fallen to the floor, and flowers have shaken vigorously in their vases, finally jumping to the floor without the aid of human hands. Once, the main ceiling support began to smoulder. Mrs Howarth called the fire-brigade, but when the beam was examined it wasn't even warm!

The Guides passed into the drawing-room and looked at a model galleon over the fire-place. Mrs Howarth related how this object flew across the room during a Christmas celebration, a phenomenon that, she declared, was witnessed by several guests.

Somewhat subdued, the Guides climbed the stairs to another "haunted" room, in which Mrs Howarth testified to seeing the brilliant figure of a monk, "and," Mrs Howarth assured the Guides, "I wasn't frightened at all." The honest Guides admitted that they would have been! How about *you*?

In the apartment known as the Priest's Room two secret hiding-places were discovered by Mrs Howarth. Sweeping the room, she accidentally hit against the wall with her brush, which went through the plaster and disclosed a priest-hole lined with wattle-and-daub; it extended back several feet, originally to John Wall's bedroom in the porch wing of the house.

In Chingle Hall ghosts don't confine themselves to haunting only under the cover of night. Mrs Howarth told the Guides that while she was preparing prizes for the annual local dog show a hooded figure in a dark habit passed her in broad daylight and walked through the porch.

If the Guides looked a little apprehensively over their shoulders as they left Chingle Hall, you will understand why if you ever go there.

Who'll Clean THEM?

Photo by Mrs. J. Keenan

With these 2nd Putney Guides it's a case of the pots calling the camp kettle black

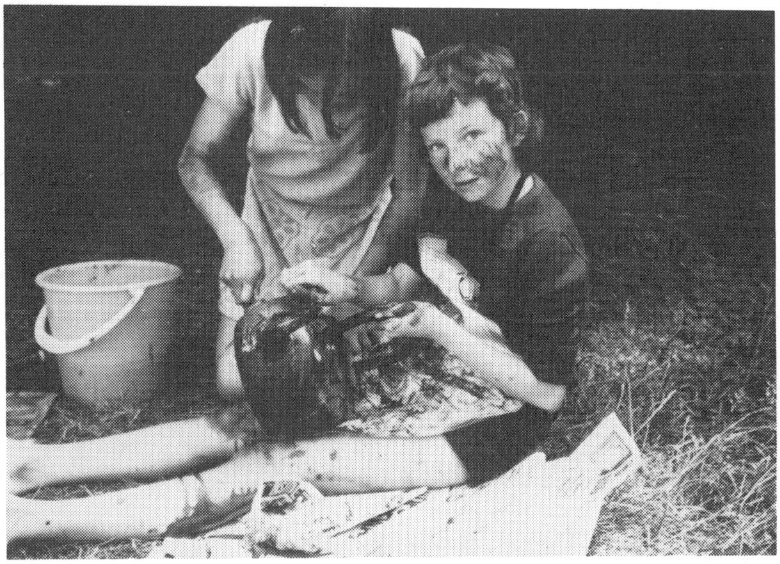

Sing~Along

Photo: Mrs. Alison Parkes

Guide entertainers from the 1st Formby (St. Peter's) Company

Up the Creek

by Jean Howard

Janet either missed the water or "caught a crab"

"Cheer up, Jan! It's Easter next week; no more school, no more prep!"

It was the last Guide meeting of the spring term and all the members of the 2nd Wallington Company were happily discussing plans for the holidays ahead—all, that is, except Janet Birch, who seemed unusually quiet as she helped her friend Katie pack away the signalling equipment in a box. Even the fact that she'd just gained the Signaller Badge didn't seem to have cheered her up. At Katie's words she tried to smile, but it was obviously an effort.

"Sorry to be such a misery. As you know, my parents are abroad, and I heard today that my mother won't be able to fly home for the holidays. I shall just have to stay here with my aunt. She's very kind, but it's not the same."

"What wretched luck! But this gives me an idea. Why not come down to Frenton with me? It's a lovely little fishing village near the mouth of the River Medway. I go there every Easter to stay with my cousin, and they've always said I can bring a friend."

All of a sudden Janet's world seemed a much brighter place, and she was soon singing Taps as cheerfully as the rest of the Guides.

Her aunt was delighted that she should have a real holiday. A few days later Tim met them at the station and drove them back to the cottage by the long winding creek that ran down to the main river.

Tim was mate on one of the Medway tugs and was often away for several days at a time, so Katie's cousin, Molly, was glad of the girls' company. Janet soon settled down happily to enjoy her holiday.

The scenery was strange at first after the noisy, built-up London suburb in which she lived. Long spits of land stretched out into the wide river-mouth, and at low tide there were miles of mudbanks where sea-gulls and curlews strutted about in search of food.

The weather was very warm for the time of year, and each day the two girls walked for miles. They made fires from driftwood on the shingle beaches and practised various ways of cooking their lunch. They would certainly have some new ideas when it was their turn to be cooks in camp in the summer.

After lunch they watched the big cargo-ships and tankers coming in round Garrison Point or heading for the open sea. Soon they could recognise the flags of other countries, and they discussed which they would choose for the Guide Friendship Badge.

One day Katie asked Tim if they could borrow his dinghy and go for a row.

"Sure you can," said Tim, "but don't go further than the old fort. The tide's pretty strong past that point, and you could have trouble getting back."

The weather had begun to change, and grey clouds were building up from the west. Wearing their navy-blue anoraks and jeans and taking sandwiches and apples for their lunch, the Guides set off, promising to be back by teatime.

Katie was an expert with the oars and had gained the Boatswain Badge the summer before. She rowed down to the little jetty by the ruined fort that had been built there many years before to keep invaders at bay. She showed Janet how to tie the dinghy up securely to the jetty with a round turn and two half-hitches, and then both girls scrambled ashore and began to explore. Both liked collecting wildflowers. They found several early specimens neither had seen before. They also found some birds' nests in the old brickwork, but were very careful not to disturb the eggs.

The sea air made them hungry, and they sat down on a pile of fallen bricks in a sheltered corner of the ruin and enjoyed their picnic. It was high tide now, and the mudbanks were hidden beneath a sheet of grey water. In the distance the Guides could see where the creek joined the wide mouth of the river, which the light wind was ruffling into small waves.

"Can I try rowing a bit after lunch?" Janet asked. "I've never done any, but it looks quite easy."

Katie hadn't the heart to say that it might look easy but that it took a lot of practice. She was rather worried about the weather, but she said, "All right, while it's slack water; but I think there's a squall coming up and we ought to be getting back soon."

They clambered back along the derelict jetty and down the rickety steps to the boat. Katie untied the rope and pushed off. Janet gripped the oars firmly and began to row upstream. At first the dinghy went round and round in circles as Janet either missed the water altogether or dug in too deep and caught a "crab". Katie became almost helpless with laughter, but Janet gradually improved and began to make her way up the creek. Suddenly, however, she caught another "crab", and the oar jumped out of her hand and slid swiftly into the water. With a cry she leant over the side to grab it, but the tide had started to turn and it carried the oar rapidly downstream.

Excitedly they climbed aboard the old craft

Katie took over and tried desperately to row with one oar, but a sudden gust of wind hit them, spinning the dinghy round, and it began to drift back the way they'd come, gathering speed as the tide ran stronger and stronger. Katie tried to pull the boat towards the shore, but the current was too strong and they were soon in sight of the long spit of land where the creek joined the river. Beyond that was the open sea!

Only one more bend and they would be at the mercy of the full force of the tide. Katie looked round desperately. She saw a battered old sailing-boat lying moored to a buoy some distance from the bank. Pulling with all her might, she managed to turn the dinghy towards it.

"Quick, Jan! I'll try to reach that boat. Grab anything you can and hang on tight! Are you ready? NOW!"

Janet leant out as far as she dared. As they brushed past, she caught at an old fender hanging over the side of the craft. She hung on grimly whilst Katie threw a rope round a broken bit of railing and tied the dinghy up securely before they could be swept out into the current again.

The girls helped each other to climb aboard. They looked round, thankful to be on something reasonably solid and safe. Janet found herself trembling with excitement or fear—she wasn't sure which! She helped Katie tug at the hatch. To their surprise, it opened quite easily, although the rest of the boat was rusty and neglected. They stepped down into a small cabin. It was stuffy and dark, but at least it was out of the wind.

"We'd better find something to tie to the mast as a distress-signal," said Katie. "There ought to be—why, what's up, Jan?"

White-faced, Janet turned to her. "Look, Katie!" she whispered. "That box—it's marked gelignite!"

Katie followed Janet's pointing finger. In a corner of the bin Janet had opened there was a variety of things, including a small box on which the sinister word GELIGNITE was painted in white.

"Gosh, what have we stumbled on?" breathed out Katie.

"It looks as if this old boat is being used for storing something illegal," said Janet. "It isn't likely that gelignite would be left here for honest purposes."

"I suppose there is gelignite inside," said Katie. "The box might be empty."

Janet didn't reply. Clearly to their ears had come the sound of an engine. Both girls ran to the porthole and looked through. A motorboat with three men aboard was coming swiftly up the creek from the sea and heading straight for the old boat.

"We'd better make ourselves scarce," said Katie, and Janet didn't argue as Katie grabbed her hand and pulled her towards a sail-locker.

"This is where the sails are stowed," she whispered. "Crawl in and keep quiet. We should be safe if the men don't look for something in here."

The motor-boat drew up alongside the old boat. Both girls prayed that their dinghy wouldn't be noticed. They heard one of the men call out above the wind, "Hurry up and collect the jelly. We'd best be away before that patrol-boat comes along. The river-police are getting nosy."

As the girls heard the men clamber aboard, they worked their way behind some large canvas bags containing sails and curled up, making themselves as small as they could. The smell of mildew assailed them, and Janet shuddered as she thought of the spiders they might disturb.

The men entered the cabin. In their cramped, suffocating quarters, the girls were able to hear all that was said. It soon became clear that the old sailing-boat was a depository for equipment, including gelignite, used in criminal activities. The three men evidently planned to break into a bank in Westham through a tobacconist's shop next door.

"Get a move on, Len," a gruff voice urged. "The weather ain't too good, and we'd better get back afore *Marianne* is missed."

"Okay! That's about all we'll need. How about bashing a couple of 'oles in the old tub next time we come?"

"She's too useful to lose. We'll lie low after this job, and hope the river-police'll forget us. Let's go!"

A few moments later there was the sound of the engine springing into life, and the girls heard the motor-boat beat away downstream.

Janet and Katie crawled out of their hiding-place, white and shaken. They were thankful that the men hadn't noticed the dinghy tied up on the other side.

The problem now was how to warn the police. It was quite

"How about 'oles in the old tub?" the girls heard a man say

possible that no one would come up the creek until the tide turned some hours later, and then it might be too late to prevent a bank robbery and apprehend the criminals.

Katie looked thoughtfully at Janet. "Look, Jan, if you could help I believe we could get the sails up and make the main river, where there would be a chance of getting help and passing on information. I've often sailed with Tim, and it would be better to try rather than sit here—perhaps all night."

Janet jumped at the chance of making herself useful. Together they managed to rig sails and haul them up to the mast-head. Then they tied the dinghy astern so that it would tow behind them. It was comforting to know it was there, just in case they had to abandon ship!

A final check all round, and they cast off from the buoy and headed out into the main channel.

"Try and keep her on this course while I see to the sails," called Katie, and Janet found herself at the helm of a sailing-boat for the first time in her life, and under what could hardly be called ideal conditions.

At first the boat seemed impossible to control, but gradually she got the feel of it, and as the sails filled in the freshening wind the boat sped gracefully out into the wide river mouth.

Katie set the boat on a course that would take them near to the shipping lanes, and then left Janet in charge while she went below to see if all was well. She emerged from the cabin looking worried.

"I'm afraid our vessel is hardly seaworthy," she said. "It doesn't surprise me, really. The force of the wind and tide have found some weak spots, and water is beginning to trickle in in several places. We must keep a sharp lookout and be ready to signal for help. With such bad visibility we might not be noticed."

She took over the helm again, and Janet clambered down into the cabin to fetch a tattered red ensign that she had noticed there. The floor was now covered with several inches of water, and she returned hastily to the cockpit, where the stinging rain lashed her face as she peered into the gloom, ready to signal the first approaching ship. She had always been keen on signalling. Tying the ensign to an old boathook, she felt equipped to prove that she had not gained the Signaller Badge in vain.

The storm that had been building up all afternoon now broke in earnest and a sudden sharp squall hit the yacht, ripping the big mainsail with a terrible rending noise. Katie fought for control as the boat heeled over at an alarming angle, hung there for a breathtaking moment, and then swung wildly back again. CRASH! The heavy boom hit Katie on the side of the head, knocking her half over the rusty safety-rail, which was all that separated her from the murky waters of the river!

Janet dived forward and grabbed her feet, pulling her back, unconscious, into the comparative safety of the cockpit. Then she grasped the helm in an effort to control the wildly flapping sails, but another violent gust of wind swept the boat sideways. There was a dull thud and a jolt,

The heavy boom hit Katie, knocking her senseless

and their deep keel stuck firmly into a hidden mudbank.

In the momentary calm that followed, Janet heard the throb of engines and saw the shadowy form of a large cargo boat passing through the grey mist. She shouted and signalled madly with her improvised flag, but the ship went on its way, unseeing.

For the first time since their adventure began, Janet felt really frightened and alone. What could she do against such odds? Then her years of training as a Brownie and a Guide came to her aid. She must keep cheerful and be prepared to signal to the next boat. A fine rain still drove in from the sea, but the wind seemed to have dropped a little. As the boat was no longer pitching so wildly, Janet was able to reach into the cabin for an old blue blanket she'd seen lying on a locker and wrap it round Katie, who was beginning to show signs of coming round.

The patrol-boat swung towards the Guides' grounded boat

Janet wrapped a blanket round Katie, who began to come round

Although they were aground, the water was still rising in the cabin, and Janet wondered how long it would be before they had to abandon ship and take to the dinghy. She drew the blanket closer round Katie, who opened her eyes and asked what was happening.

Janet reassured her that all would be well, and said she was just waiting for a boat to come by. To keep up their spirits, she began to sing one of her favourite camp-songs:—

"Did you ever, ever, ever in your long long life
See a long-legged sailor with a long-legged wife?"

She had just started the third verse when out of the gloom came a blue-and-white motorboat. On its side were the words *MEDWAY PATROL.*

Frantically Janet signalled an urgent message for help—three dots, three dashes, three dots. SOS, SOS, she signalled again and again in Morse. The patrol-boat seemed to hold its course; then slowly it swung round towards the grounded boat.

In a short time the Guides were helped on board the patrol-boat and told their strange story.

A radio message was sent at once to the Westham police, who assured the river-police that a trap would be set and the robbers caught.

Leaving a marker-buoy in case the old boat sank in the night and became a danger to shipping, the patrol-boat turned for port, towing Tim's dinghy behind it. Katie was already recovering in the warm cabin, and was full of praise for the way Janet had acted.

Janet laughed. "It is certainly useful to know Morse, but the first thing I aim to do when I get home is to go to the boating centre and learn how to ROW!"

What Do You Know about FLAGS?

asks L. Baker

The World Flag of the Association of Girl Guides and Girl Scouts

A flag can be divided into four quarters. The one on the upper left next to the flagpole is called the *canton*. In it special emblems may appear—for example, the fifty stars of the American flag.

The background against which these emblems are set is called the *field*. The field can also be used to describe any part of the flag on which emblems or designs are placed.

Emblems themselves are called *charges*. The Union Flag is charged with three crosses on a blue field.

The part of the flag nearest the flagpole is the *hoist*, the part farthest away is the *fly*.

A national flag is a flag for the whole country. Some countries have state or government flags in addition to the national one.

Late in the Middle Ages a set of rules developed for flags. Each nobleman had his own flag. In England its size depended on his rank. An emperor's flag was six feet square, a king's five feet square, and so on down through dukes, earls and others to the knights, who were only allowed to carry triangular pennants.

Military flags are called *colours*.

On certain special occasions a ship will display all flags, when sailors say the ship is "dressed". A ship wears her flags, never flies them. A ship in a port may wear two flags: the flag of her own country, at the stern, and on her mast the flag of the country she is visiting. When a merchant ship leaves port she sometimes wears the flag of the country she is going to visit. She may also wear a house flag, which is the flag of the company who owns her.

A special naval flag is called a *jack*. It is worn on the jackstaff on the bow of a ship.

Great Britain's national flag is usually called the Union Jack, but this term is only really correct when the flag is on the jackstaff of a naval vessel. The proper name is the Union Flag.

An *ensign* is a special flag worn on the stern of a warship. In the middle ages a nobleman commanding a warship would hang his personal flag from the stern for identification. Nowadays it identifies the country from which the naval vessel has come. Great Britain and some other countries have ensigns that are distinct from their national flag.

Striking or hauling down the ensign during a battle is a sign of surrender. Commanders of British warships have been known to go into battle with two or three ensigns to ensure that if one was shot away there would be another to take its place and so avoid any suggestion of a surrender signal.

There is a long tradition behind the use of red flags for defiance. Years ago red was considered to stand for bravery and aggression. In Roman times it was the symbol of combat. By raising a red flag or standard above his tent, a Roman general told his troops to prepare for battle.

Frenchmen of Normandy raised red streamers on their vessels in the thirteenth century when they were about to engage in combat with ships from England. In the seventeenth and eighteenth centuries red was the pirate colour in common use on the high seas.

In France, at about this time, if a government declared an emergency a red flag was raised as a sign that peacetime laws were suspended and that the armed forces were taking over control.

A red flag was raised during the French Revolution and became the symbol of revolution. It became that in Russia and later in China. Socialists adopted it as their flag, and it became the flag of the Labour Party in Great Britain.

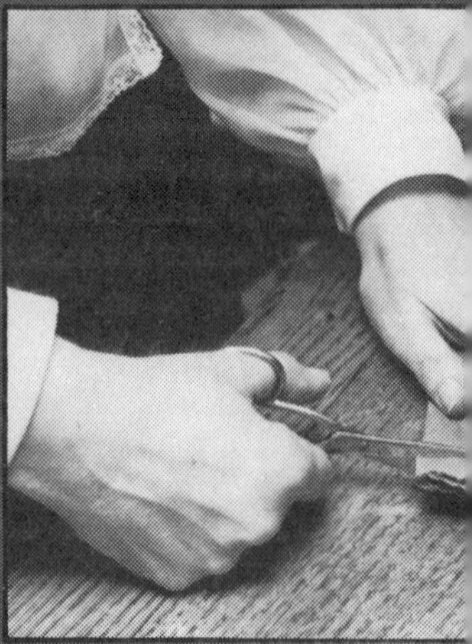

Make a Bunc

Phyllis Mead Shows You How

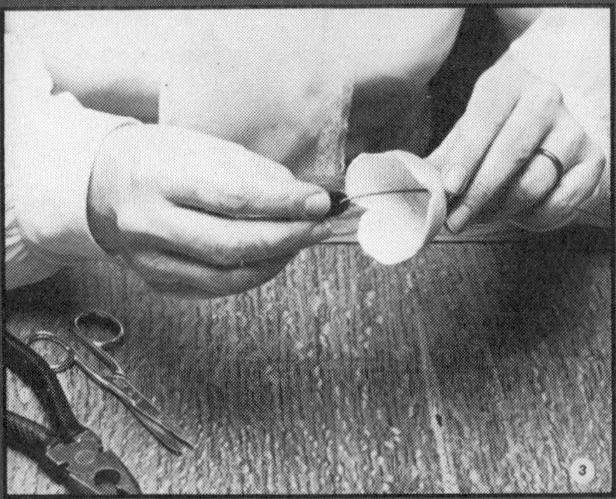

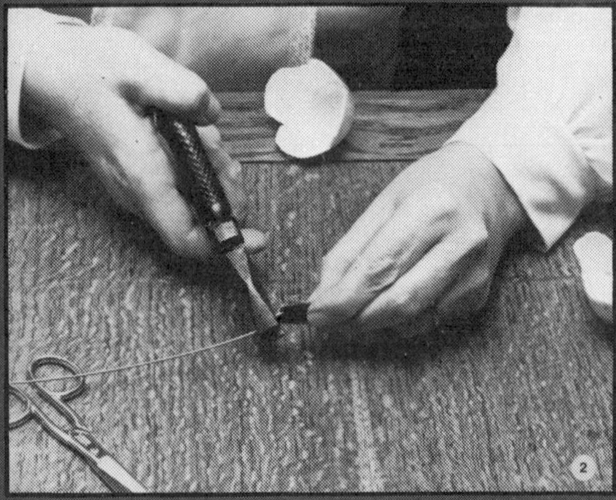

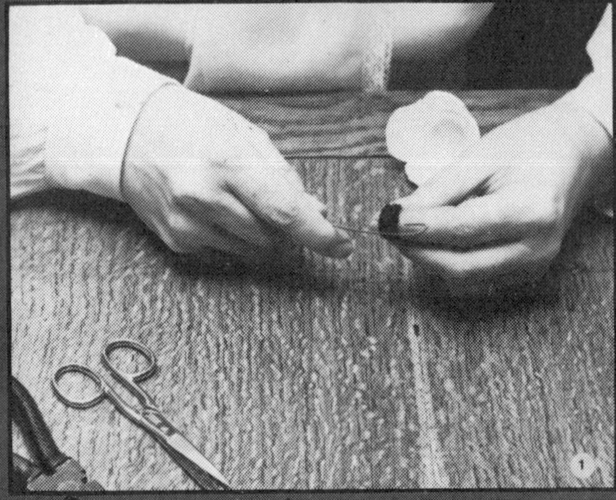

You will need a polystyrene egg-carton, wire, black yarn, green crepe paper, modelling clay, glue, scissors, pliers, a ruler.

Carefully cut one cup from the base of the egg-carton. Cut out four small "V" shapes, equally spaced, round the top of the cup. Trim the petals thus formed into shape.

Take a piece of wire 30cm ($11\frac{3}{4}$") long and shape a small hook at one end. Wind a length of black yarn round one finger six times. Slip the wire hook through the yarn loop (*photograph 1*).

Pinch the hook with the pliers to hold yarn in place (*photograph 2*). Trim off any surplus yarn. Thread the tulip head on to the wire (*photograph 3*). Secure with a small piece of modelling clay at the top of the stalk (*photograph 4*).

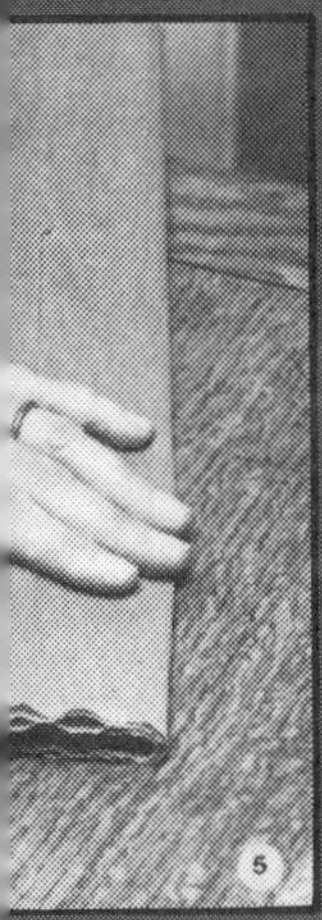

... of Tulips

...ords and Photographs

Fig. 7

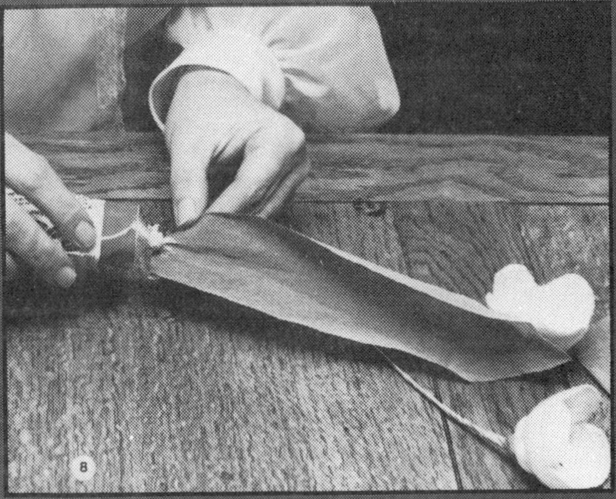

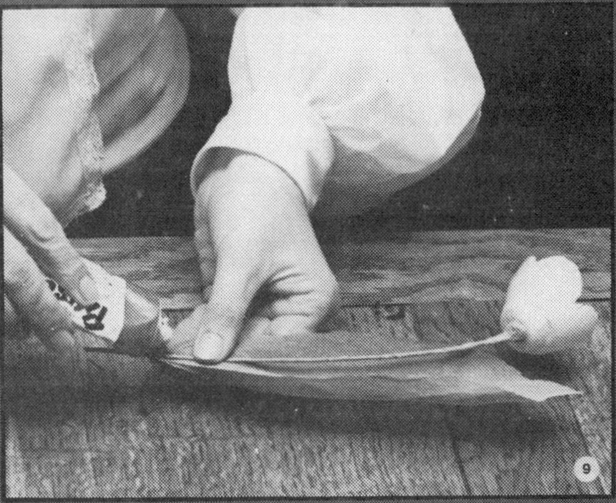

Cut a strip of crepe paper 2cm ($\frac{3}{4}$") wide along the length of your paper (*photograph 5*). This should be twice the length of the stalk wire. Attach the paper to the wire by pressing it firmly round the modelling clay. Cover the wire by twisting it between the thumb and forefinger of your right hand while holding the strip of paper in the left hand (*photograph 6*). The paper should be stretched gently and should overlap the previous layer. At the bottom of the stalk trim off any surplus paper and fix with a spot of glue.

Cut out two leaves (*figure 7*) across the width of the paper. Stretch the centre of each leaf slightly by pulling gently between your thumbs. Pleat the base of each leaf and fix with a little glue (*photograph 8*).

Attach the leaves on opposite sides, but at the same distance from the bottom of the stalk with glue (*photographs 9 and 10*).

CHRISTMAS CUSTOMS

by Gary Keene and Neville Randall

MIDDLE AGES. BISHOP NICHOLAS OF MYRA BECAME A LEGENDARY SAINT. REWARDING GOOD DUTCH CHILDREN WITH PRESENTS, PUNISHING BAD ONES, IN DECEMBER. NICKNAMED SINTER KLAAS.
DUTCH SETTLERS TOOK HIS LEGEND TO AMERICA. MERGED HIM WITH SCANDINAVIANS' NORSE GOD ODIN AS SANTA CLAUS. BRINGING PRESENTS ON SLEIGHS DRAWN BY REINDEER FROM FROZEN NORTH.
VISUALISED BY 19TH CENTURY CARTOONIST THOMAS NAST.
HIS DRAWINGS REVIVED ANOTHER NICHOLAS GOOD DEED. TO AVOID BEING SEEN, HE DROPPED A PURSE DOWN A CHIMNEY. IT FELL IN A STOCKING HUNG UP TO DRY.
THE FATHER CHRISTMAS LEGEND WAS COMPLETE.
A.D. 597. ST. AUGUSTINE LANDED ON THANET. TO CONVERT BRITAIN TO CHRISTIANITY. FOUND ANGLES AND SAXONS ROASTING OXEN TO CELEBRATE YULE. THE FEAST WAS TAKEN OVER BY CHRISTMAS.
MEDIEVAL DECEMBER. FORESTS WERE HUNTED FOR WILD BOAR. TO PROVIDE BOAR'S HEAD FOR NOBLES' CHRISTMAS FEASTS. FOLLOWED, WHEN EXTINCT, BY PEACOCK, GOOSE AND SWAN.
TUDOR BRITAIN. THE LORD OF THE MANOR SAT ON A RAISED PLATFORM, SURROUNDED BY FAMILY, ATTENDANTS AND FRIENDS. TRUMPET FANFARES ANNOUNCED SUCCESSIVE COURSES — OF AN EIGHT-HOUR CHRISTMAS DINNER.
1492. CHRISTOPHER COLUMBUS DISCOVERED AMERICA. RETURNED WITH TOBACCO, POTATOES AND A BIRD HE CALLED INDIAN FOWL. SOON BRED IN BRITAIN TO PROVIDE CHRISTMAS DINNER FOR THE RICH.
EVERYONE ATE PIES. OF MINCED MUTTON AND OX TONGUE. BAKED LIKE A MANGER. TO HOLD A DOUGHY JESUS DOLL.
BANNED BY CROMWELL. RETURNED WITH THE RESTORATION SMALL, ROUND, FILLED WITH PRESERVED FRUIT. STILL CALLED MINCE PIE.
15TH CENTURY CHRISTMAS DISHES INCLUDED FRUMENTY. WHEAT BOILED IN MILK. WITH EGGS, SPICES, DRIED PLUMS AND MEAT LUMPS. PLUM PORRIDGE.
STIFFENED AROUND 1620 INTO MEATLESS PLUM OR CHRISTMAS PUDDING.
A.D. 720. CHRISTMAS EVE IN GERMANY. ST. BONIFACE, HOLY MAN FROM BRITAIN, FOUND PAGAN WORSHIPPERS ABOUT TO SACRIFICE A BOY BENEATH AN OAK.
HE RESCUED THE BOY, CUT DOWN THE OAK, REVEALED A LITTLE FIR.
"FROM THIS NIGHT THAT LITTLE FIR SHALL BE YOUR EMBLEM. IT IS THE SIGN OF ETERNAL LIFE, FOR ITS LEAVES ARE EVER GREEN. IT POINTS TO HEAVEN AND SHALL HENCEFORTH BE CALLED THE TREE OF THE CHRIST CHILD."
1841. PRINCE ALBERT, QUEEN VICTORIA'S GERMAN HUSBAND, RECALLED HIS FAMILY CHRISTMASSES. SET UP A CHRISTMAS TREE AT WINDSOR. AND STARTED A BRITISH INSTITUTION.
PRE-CHRISTIAN JERUSALEM. JEWS HELD A FESTIVAL TO CELEBRATE THE REDEDICATION OF SOLOMON'S TEMPLE. LIT CANDLES AS AN EMBLEM OF TRUTH.
1530. A GERMAN CHRISTMAS EVE. MARTIN LUTHER TOLD HIS FAMILY OF BETHLEHEM'S STARRY SKY. DASHED OUTSIDE AND TIED CANDLES TO THE BRANCHES OF A TINY FIR.
GERMANS, LATER BRITONS, TIED THEM TO THEIR CHRISTMAS TREES.
1878. NEWCASTLE. JOSEPH SWAN INVENTED AN INCANDESCENT ELECTRIC BULB. CHRISTMAS TREE CANDLES WERE REPLACED BY SAFER, MORE DECORATIVE COLOURED CHRISTMAS LIGHTS.

Published by arrangement with the Daily Mail, London.

CONTRIBUTIONS THANKFULLY RECEIVED

Short, complete Guiding stories, articles, novel puzzles, how-to-makes, and pictures in black-and-white or colour of Guiding activities are welcome throughout the year. All should link up with some aspect of Guiding. Send with stamped and fully addressed envelope for reply to ROBERT MOSS, EDITOR, THE GIRL GUIDE ANNUAL, GREEN ACRES, KIDNAPPERS' LANE, CHELTENHAM, GLOS., GL53 0NP. Payment of accepted material is made soon after acceptance.

GIRL GUIDES

Collect Coloured Glass

LESLIE DOE Offers Hints on Making an Unusual Collection

When you go out hiking in the country, or walk along footpaths and in the park or at the seaside, keep your eyes open for broken pieces of glass. You may find enough to begin a collection. Other places to look are beside rivers and canals, under hedges in the country, on newly ploughed land, near rubbish dumps, on waste ground, and near footpaths almost anywhere.

Small coloured pieces are the best to look for, and choose flattish pieces if possible. When you get home, wash the pieces carefully and let them dry. Select the best ones for your collection—you need two or three pieces of each tint or colour and, of course, as many different colours as possible. Browns, dark-greens and yellow are easy to find; they belong to old beer and wine bottles. Dark-blues are also easy to acquire, as they come from chemists' poison bottles. Light-blues come from old medicine bottles and reds from red tail-lamps of cars or even from beautiful Venetian red wine-glasses and bowls.

You may be tempted to include pieces of plastic that are pretty, but it's better to keep to "glass only".

The pieces should not be too large, but any that are worth showing can be made smaller by wrapping in newspaper or cloth and tapping with a hammer. Be *very careful* if you do this, as newly broken glass has very sharp edges; the small pieces already broken that you find lying on the ground will have less sharp edges, but obviously these too must be handled sensibly. Incidentally, besides making an interesting collection you will be performing a community service by removing glass pieces that might cause fires.

When you think you have enough pieces, mount them on sheets of white cardboard, using a transparent adhesive: "UHU" is very satisfactory. Any pieces that are curved should be stuck on with the rounded side downwards. Colours can be kept separate—that is, one card for blues, one for reds, one for browns, and so on.

Put the cards into a suitable box, which you can decorate as you wish. Show it to your Patrol and Company. It will be surprising if such an unusual and pretty collection doesn't excite general admiration.

Save the Village

Patrol Purpose Plan

Village ponds in Britain are disappearing at the rate of 5,000 a year. What a loss this is! And what a wonderful project for your Patrol—clearing out and restoring a village pond!

It's not an easy job, and not a very clean one. Weeds will have to be cleared out, but pretty certainly the pond will be choked with less pleasant items, such as rusty bedstead bits, broken bottles, mud to a considerable depth, rotten vegetation, and a

Well-preserved bottles are among the "treasures" likely to be found in an old pond

Photos by Alan Band Associates

Pond

Volunteers begin the task of clearing out weeds and debris from a village pond

variety of household objects that may have disappeared under the water many years before.

This may well be a long-term project, for your pond may have been silted up for very many years, and restoring it to a condition where it will be a delight to the eye and a fit habitation for fish and wildfowl may demand real dedication. But what a reward awaits you when residents and visitors see it once again as a "living pond"!

A campaign to save village ponds run by a national newspaper some years ago resulted in a number being restored or improved. Villagers of Four Marks, in Hampshire, worked together to clear their pond of the deposits of many years, and in the process they brought to light an astonishing number of unexpected objects, including a few that could be classed as "treasures". Perhaps you will make rewarding discoveries too. The Four Marks excavators unearthed Stone Age implements, Roman pottery, antique bottles and jars, which were snapped up by collectors for a good price, and—most surprising of all—a woman's century-old riding-cloak made of rich green felt. A local legend told of a phantom horse and cart that vanished into the pond in far-off days. From the pond the villagers pulled a harness, a blinker and a bridle, a wooden cart-shaft, and then exposed—wait for it!—the bones of a drowned horse!

You may not make discoveries quite as exciting, but, on the other hand, you may bring to light something that makes the front pages of the national newspapers. Whatever you do or do not find, one thing is certain, you will be making a fine contribution to the village and the countryside.

Even if your local pond doesn't need "saving" it may well be that you can devise a Patrol Purpose Plan designed to beautify and generally improve it.

The hundred-year-old lady's riding cloak found in the pond at Four Marks, Hampshire

A Grave Challenge

The back as well as the front ▲ of a headstone may have an interesting inscription

The Guides really needed a ▶ scythe to reach these headstones

Written and illustrated by Muriel E. Florentine

Camping in the beautiful Northumbrian countryside, Guides of the 7th Monkseaton Company undertook an unusual Patrol Challenge. Each Patrol were given a question-sheet based on the ancient St. Cuthbert's Church, in the tiny village of Bellingham.

On a blazing August morning, the Guides began to discover many interesting things in the overgrown churchyard.

An enormous yew on the north side was bound around with iron bands and was found to be nine hundred years old, one of the oldest yews in the country. Such trees were originally planted as a form of protection for the church. This one shielded St. Cuthbert's from the full onslaught of fierce north winds, the church being very exposed to the Tyne valley.

The Guides found curious epitaphs on the headstones. They soon realised that these revealed much social and local history, including the intermarriage of local families, and recorded the large families that were common in earlier days, the high proportion of infants who died before reaching the age of two, and the deaths of local people in far-away countries, which reflected the occurrence of wars and emigration. Changes in the English language were noted in the spelling and the different use of words. Farmhouses and other dwellings mentioned on the headstones were traced by the Guides on the latest Ordnance Survey maps of the area.

The epitaphs were found on the backs as well as the fronts of the headstones. These were mostly solemn and rather dramatic, rather than humorous. The strong social divisions of the past were clearly illustrated by the large and often elaborate headstones and tombs of the landowners and wealthy merchants in comparison with the plain graves of labourers. In Bellingham the Guides saw a private walled-off, gated plot of land for the Bowes-Lyon family, ancestors and relatives of the Queen Mother.

Investigation of the churchyard ended with a session of headstone rubbing. The Guides used rolls of greaseproof paper held in place with masking-tape and carefully rubbed with heelball. Some excellent rubbings were obtained, and the Guides agreed that it could have been extended into an activity of its own. The rubbings revealed the skill of the stonemasons in the ornate lettering and decorative borders and symbols. Some headstones were badly weathered, and the lettering needed very careful deciphering.

The Guides returned to camp well pleased with their day out. They all agreed that the Challenge had proved to be a fascinating and rewarding one. Several decided to extend the project to make it the basis from which to work for the Local History badge. Why don't you try this? If you find a churchyard worth investigating, don't forget to ask permission to work in it.

▲ Rubbing needed great concentration and care

◀ Someone looking critically on may or may not be a help

GUIDE GAMES

Problems and Puzzles

THE SPIDER'S WEB

by Brenda Morton

This Patrol activity is an amusing form of Kim's game. Where are the flies on the spider's web?

Each Guide in the Patrol needs her own web and three flies. Draw the web as shown in the diagram on a large sheet of paper, with the spider in the middle. Black buttons or beads will do for flies, but funny ones can be quickly made.

A small oval shape in black cardboard has three short pieces of black thread laid across the back of it and fixed with a strip of sticky tape to make a little black fly with three legs at each side of the body.

The first player lays her flies on her web. She can lay them on the open spaces, on the strands, or on junctions. The other players look at it for a few seconds—say ten. It is then covered up, and they try to place their flies on the same positions on their own webs.

Are they correct? Players take turns to set the flies for the others to try and match.

KIM'S GAME IN PICTURES

by Rosalie Brown

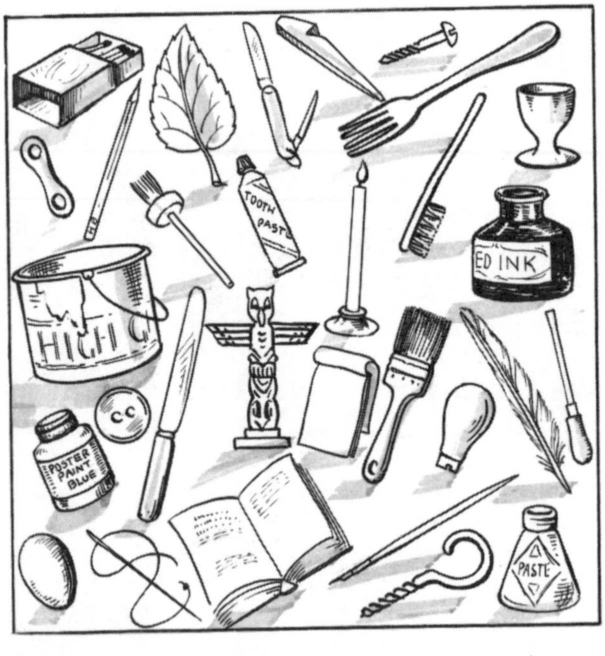

Here's an interesting test of observation and memory. Study the objects in the drawing for one minute and cover up. How many can you remember? Keep them covered and answer these questions:—

1. Was the matchbox a full one?
2. Had the screw a round head or a countersunk one?
3. How many holes were there in the button?
4. How many blades were in the penknife?
5. Was the candle lit?
6. What colour was the poster-paint?
7. Was the needle threaded? If so, was the cotton knotted?
8. How many faces were there on the totem?
9. Was the ink-bottle corked?
10. Had the leaf a smooth or serrated edge?
11. Was the pencil a hard or a soft one?
12. What else had two holes in it?

MESSAGE IN TIME

by Daphne M. Pilcher

Your clue is that 3 o'clock is J. Take away the clock numbers and just leave the hands—does that make it easier?

Here is the message:

3.40 2.10 5.25 7.5
2.10 10.55 11.00
10.55 6.35 8.20
8.45 2.10
9.20 2.10 9.15 9.40
8.50 1.50 9.20

WORD HUNT

B	D	E	F	A	R	Z	O	G	O	G	S
M	A	H	R	O	W	A	R	I	E	U	K
T	I	D	I	D	C	K	N	R	J	I	I
E	L	F	E	T	A	O	R	L	R	D	L
N	D	H	N	N	M	C	A	G	A	E	L
D	F	N	D	I	P	H	O	U	W	R	S
E	J	N	S	V	Y	O	X	I	G	Z	I
R	K	E	U	Z	M	T	W	D	H	A	P
F	N	O	Y	V	U	G	H	E	F	E	B
O	O	P	H	N	P	S	M	S	L	E	R
O	T	F	U	N	V	K	Z	R	F	L	P
T	S	D	O	U	P	A	R	T	I	E	S
G	L	Q	T	W	F	X	B	D	I	D	S
W	X	R	Q	Y	L	B	A	D	G	E	S
K	M	S	J	A	T	B	B	E	L	J	Q
P	A	T	R	O	L	S	C	K	C	H	C

Jill Blakeley, a Canadian Guide of Toronto, invites you to find the following words in this Word Hunt.

The words may go diagonally, across, or down: BADEN POWELL, PATROLS, GIRL GUIDES, FUN, KNOTS, CAMP, BADGES, SKILL, PARTIES, FRIENDS

SCAVENGER HUNT With a Difference

by Daphne M. Pilcher

This is an ideal nature hunt for camp. You will need a plastic container and an ability to solve the clues given below so that you will know what you have to scavenge.

1. What a drowning man will clutch at
2. What makes fine birds
3. What you can't get blood from
4. When this is out of bloom, kissing is out of season
5. You may take a horse to this, but you can't make him drink
6. What the early bird catches
7. What's greener on the other side of the fence
8. There are no birds in last year's one
9. There is no rose without it
10. What a rolling stone doesn't gather

CAMPING

The scrambling net presents a tough challenge for the 9th Clapham Park Company Guide attempting the assault course at camp

Colour print by Mrs J. Barclay

There are easier ways of crossing a stream, but not as much fun for the Guides of the 13th Hackney Company at camp

Colour print by Mrs S. L. Gordon

"Red men" round the camp-fire—the 43rd Exeter Company (St. Sidwell's)

Colour print by Miss V. A. Down

DAYS

"I'll wash that dirt right out of your hair," Alison Gell tells her P. L., Amanda Rayner, as she starts shampooing operations at the 2nd Marske-by-Sea Company's camp

Colour print by Amanda Rayner

"Come and get it!" A quartet of neat and efficient cooks ready to serve lunch to the 9th Clapham Park Company at camp

Colour print by Mrs J. Barclay

Salad for lunch for the 3rd Headstone Company, Harrow, at camp—and it's voted very nice too

Colour print by Mrs L. J. Field

Camp Magic

A playlet in one scene, suitable for acting at camp—out of doors or indoors

by A. L. DUNCAN

CHARACTERS

		Miss Tent	**Voices heard but not seen**
		Miss Flag	**OR**
		Mr. Poles	**Guides dressed to represent**
Jill	**Patrol Leader**	**Mr. Mallet**	**"spirits" of these items: i.e.**
Kate	**Patrol Second**	**Mr. Bedroll**	**green top and tights for**
Jo	**lazy Guide**	**Miss Dixie**	**Miss Tent, brown for Pegs, tinfoil**
Penny and Pat	**Guides**	**Misses Pegs**	**for Miss Dixie, etc, etc.**

SCENE

A Patrol Camp Permit site at the end of a Permit test. Site is untidy, with a badly folded tent, dirty pegs and dixie, flagpole with a badly hoisted flag, a mallet, and a carelessly rolled bedroll. Kate, Penny and Pat are wiping some plastic buckets and basins

Jo (wiping her brow):
Gosh, I'm hot! I think I'll take a rest now.

Kate:
You shouldn't need a rest; you've done nothing yet. Do get a move on. Jill will be back soon and expect us to have most of the clearing-up done.

Jo:
It's all very well for Jill. She knew what she was doing—using Tina as an excuse to get away from all this clearing-up.

Pat:
Oh, Jo, you know that is not true. Jill isn't like that at all; she always works harder than any of us, especially this weekend.

Jo:
Well, so she jolly well should—she's the one getting the Patrol Camp Permit, not us.

Kate:
Oh, do shut up, Jo. You know very well the Permit is for us all, and Jill had to take Tina to meet her parents to explain to them how she broke her finger.

Jo:
Anyway, what's all the fuss about? Most of this equipment is our own and we can clean it up when we get it home, can't we?

Penny:
You know very well we can't. Miss Pritchard will be along to check the site and equipment, and if it's unsatisfactory she won't pass it.

Pat:
And then Jill won't get her Permit and we won't be able to go off for any weekend camps.

Kate:
Never mind Jo, Pat; she always likes to moan. Let's get this clean equipment over to the store hut to be checked. And, Jo, for goodness' sake do make an effort to get this place tidy. Fold that tent properly. Those poles are a disgrace. Call yourself a camper!

Kate and the two younger Guides go off carrying buckets and basin, and Jo is left on her own.

Jo (muttering to herself as she flings herself on to the ground with her head on her bedroll):
Oh, shut up, the lot of you! All I can hear is work, work, work. All weekend it's been the same—get water, get wood, wash the milk-bottles, stir the stew. It's enough to tire one out. I'll just have a quick five minutes' rest before the others return. Don't see why I should have to tidy this place up on my own. Don't really see much wrong with it, anyway.

Jo closes her eyes and yawns a couple of times before she dozes off.

Miss Tent (with a groan):
Oh, I do wish any of those other Guides had folded me up. That MADAM lying there has just bundled me into my bag. My guylines are in an appalling state.

Mr. Poles (in a gruff, surly tone):
My dear Miss Tent, I know exactly how you feel. Just look at me, tied—if you could call it tied—in the middle like a bundle of firewood. If anyone tries to lift me as I am now I'll get all twisted and slip all over the place. Oh, the pain it will cause doesn't bear thinking about!

Miss Flag (in an angry voice):
That—that—that PERSON! Mr. Poles, I just can't bring myself to call her a Guide. She's a lazy, careless, good-for-nothing. Just look at ME. I ask you! Am I at half-mast or not? She never hoists me properly, and look at the length of halyard she has left hanging out above my toggle! What is more, if she has tied me with proper knots I'll eat my own flagpole!

Mr. Mallet:
Proper knots, Miss Flag! That child doesn't know one knot from another. I'd be very much surprised if she had even heard of a clovehitch and a sheetbend, never mind be able to tie them. Just look where she threw me! I might as well be an old piece of wood instead of an important mallet. If it's left to her I'll never get back into the tent-bag—I'll just be left behind to rot away.

Miss Dixie (in a soft voice):
Oh, dear, Mr. Mallet, I do hope not! But she really is careless; look how she has left me. Instead of being a nice shiny dixie I'm only half cleaned—just like you, Misses Pegs.

Misses Pegs (3 or 4 voices gloomily together):
Yes, indeed, Miss Dixie; just look at us! Clean? She doesn't know the meaning of the word. Her camping skills are non-existent.

Miss Dixie:
I pity the Patrol Leader, and in fact the whole Patrol. They would be better off without her.

Miss Tent (getting really annoyed and worked up):
Indeed, indeed, Miss Dixie, how right you are! She is nothing but a disagreeable, unwilling, discontented, lazy, untidy, awkward, nasty . . .

Mr. Mallet (interrupting):
Oh, now, Miss Tent, don't go getting yourself so worked up! I don't think she can be as bad as all that.

Misses Pegs:
She is, she is, Mr. Mallet! Miss Tent is quite right. She is a horrid girl!

Mr. Bedroll (in a deep, lazy voice):
I'm afraid I have to agree with the Misses Pegs, and I know her better than most of you, as I am her own personal bedroll. I have suffered from her carelessness for a long time now. Do you know when we get home I shall immediately be dumped into a dark loft without so much as an airing.

Jo begins to move. She yawns and stretches her arms above her head slowly, then sits up and looks around her.

Jo:
Goodness, am I alone? I thought I had company. I must have been dreaming. But what a nasty dream—with all those horrid things said about me! Am I really like that? *She looks around her.* Gosh, what a mess! Funny! I don't remember noticing before how untidy everything is. I had better get a move on before the others return. Can't have them saying or thinking nasty things about me as well.

Jo starts tidying the tent into the bag, and tying the poles, just as the others return with Jill, the Patrol Leader.

Jill:
Good for you, Jo! I see you are working hard. Sorry I had to go off and leave you all to do the clearing-up. I'm sure you thought it was just an excuse to get away.

Jo (shamefacedly):
Oh, no, Jill; of course not!

The others look at each other and grin.

Penny and Pat:
Gosh, what has suddenly changed Jo?

Kate:
Good for you, Jo! I didn't expect this. I thought you were on strike.

Jo (continuing to tidy the site):
I was only joking, Kate. Everybody must pull their weight at a Patrol camp. Can you see to the flagpole while I take Miss Dix—er—I mean this dixie away and give it a good clean? Oh, and don't forget Mr. Mallet, will you?

Penny:
Miss Dixie and *Mr.* Mallet—what is she on about?

Pat:
I think she must have gone bonkers. Too much rest maybe and not enough work.

Jill:
No, girls, I think perhaps she has had a touch of camp magic. It can happen, you know.

Kate and Jill smile at each other.

Penny (to Pat):
Everybody seems to be bonkers here—except us, of course. Camp magic!

Pat:
Well, if it can improve people as it seems to have Jo, then I say three cheers for good old camp magic!

The End

ADVENTURE

Colour slide by Robert Moss

A short but thrilling ride on the aerial railway at Cowley Deer Park, the beautiful centre for the Guides of the county of Gloucester

It isn't exactly the height of boating luxury, but an improvised raft is tremendous fun—and so is a rope-bridge

Colour slides by Mrs E. Aveton

DAYS

Ready for the water—two Guide canoeists camping at Cowley Deer Park, where the lake provides safe canoeing and rafting

Colour slide by Robert Moss

It's thrilling, but you do need a head for heights if you go mountaineering. These are members of the Shrewsbury Scout and Guide mountaineering group

Codes, Signs and Signals

Crossword Puzzle

by Jeanelle Dening-Smitherman

How much do you know about codes, signs and signals? Find out by starting at number one, and working your way around the spiral. The last letter of each answer is the first letter of the next.

CLUES

1. Pistol used for firing flares (4)
2. ——— cross on red square means landing is prohibited on airfield (6)
3. The acknowledgment for a red flare is a ——— one (5)
4. Like the code, it was also invented by Samuel Morse (8,9)
5. "H" begins this place of call, but is not sounded (5)
6. Aldis ——— are used by ships for signalling (5)
7. Visual method of signalling with flags (9)
8. The letter "E" begins this repeat sound (4)
9. A smoke signal—this colour indicates a vessel in distress (6)
10. Six "E's" in Morse Code is the ——— signal (5)
11. If hoisted upside-down, indicates a vessel in distress (6)
12. International Distress Flags used at sea (1.1.)
13. Shape of starboard-hand buoys in the U.K. (7)
14. Red-and-yellow beach-flag indicates area patrolled by these (4-6)
15. Side of green navigation light (9)
16. Red flag on beach means bathing is ——— (9)
17. . . . — — — . . . (1,1,1)

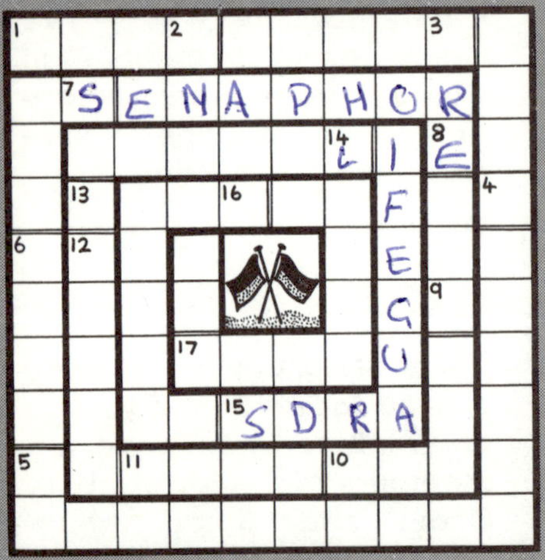

Hide-and-Seek Code Puzzle

by Jean Howard

Judy told the rest of the Patrol that she was sure that she could lay a track that they could follow, but that they would be unable to find her at the end of it!

They gave her a good start and then set off.

At first her tracking signs led through a gate, across several fields and down a narrow path through a spruce-wood, where it was more difficult to follow. Then the signs led them out of the wood into a lane with trees and a high fence on either side, and here the signs suddenly stopped. There wasn't even a footmark to be seen—only an arrow pointing to a small stick pushed into the muddy ground with a piece of paper stuck on it.

This is the message they found, and if you can read it you will be able to find Judy.

—•• ——— —• — | •—•• ——— ——— —•— | •— — | — •••• • |
——• •—• ——— ••— —• —•• |
—••• ••— — | ••— •——• | •— —• —•• | •— •—• ——— ••— —• —•• |
——— •••— • •—• •••• • •— —•• | — •••• • •—• • ••• |
•— | —••• ——— ••— ——• •••• |
••• ——— | •——— ••— —— •——• | ••—• ——— •—• |
•• — | —• ——— •—— |
— •••• • —• | • • •—— •• —• ——• | •• —• — ——— |
— •••• • | — •—• • • |
•—— •••• • •—• • | —•—— ——— ••— •—•• •—•• |
••• ••— •—• • •—•• —•—— | ••—• •• —• —•• | ——•

Winter Camping
Canadian Style

by Harriet A. Edmond

The Guides of 3rd Circle Pine Company of the Canadian Forces Base, Borden, in Ontario, Canada, learned to camp the hard way during their first year in Guides.

In temperatures well below 0°C and in snow up to ten feet deep, the girls donned snowshoes and hiked into the woods to find suitable spots to spend the night.

The Company didn't take tents on their weekend camps. Instead, the Guides zippered three groundsheets together, making a triangle, then attached the top between two trees, making what their fathers would call "hootchies". For comfort in sleeping and to raise themselves off the snow, the girls inflated military air-mattresses and placed them on the floor of their shelter. Arctic sleeping-bags and long underwear kept them warm and cosy overnight.

Mealtimes were a challenge as firelighting in deep snow is an art—one which the Guides learned in a hurry. Aluminium foil as a base made all the difference in getting fires going, and it didn't take long to find out that the dryest twigs and branches are to be found still attached to trees.

The average age of the Guides who camped in the snow on several weekends during the winter was eleven years.

Three Canadian Guides of the 3rd Pine Circle Company outside the "hootchie" they have built in the woods

The three Guiders who took the Guides on their winter camps stand on snowshoes behind the shelter in which they slept

“Oh, deer, are you going to bite?” Don’t worry, he’s only asking for food, even if his antlers look rather formidable

Colour slide of 7th Monkseaton (St. Andrew’s) Guides by Mrs M. E. Florentine

Happy Snaps

This happy group of cosmopolitans, including Arabs and Red Indians, are 1st Tunbridge Wells Guides dressed up at camp

Colour slide by Miss Daphne M. Pilcher

An attractive display created by Guides of the 1st Furze Platt Company, Maidenhead, working for the Queen's Guide badge

Colour slide by David Holland

On Show

Altrincham (Cheshire) Guides turn out in force for a local festival and make an impressive spectacle

Colour slide by Mrs J. Ward

Camping DO'S and DON'TS

by Rikki Taylor

1. When your Patrol goes off to camp,
Don't choose a site that's low and damp
Nor under trees, but in the clear,
Where falling branches cause no fear.

2. Though you may have to search around,
See that your tent's on level ground,
Or else you'll surely roll about
In sleeping-bags when lights are out.

3. Look out for anthills with great care,
Or you'll be moaning in despair
When all those busy little ants
Manage to get inside your pants!

4. Don't camp close to a stagnant pond,
Though of water you may be fond,
For you will find that if you do
Mosquitos make a meal of you.

5. If guy-ropes are not taut and firm
'Neath fallen canvas you will squirm,
But slacken them if comes the rain,
Or else it may come down again!

6. You've had a singsong round the fire;
But cover it e'er you retire,
For you won't think it is a joke
If all the camp goes up in smoke!

Guiding in the Viking Isles

Written and photographed by MICHAEL EDWARDS

What is Guiding like in a land where there are no woods or forests, and where in summer it never really gets dark? This place is so far north that you can read a book at midnight or take photographs without artificial light.

It isn't abroad. It is the islands of Shetland, Britain's northernmost county.

The Viking Isles, as the Shetland group is sometimes called, is situated one hundred miles north of John o' Groats, which puts it on the same geographical latitude as shivering Alaska and Cape Farewell. Cold and wet, you might think, but you would be wrong. Because it is bordered by the Gulf Stream, the isles of Shetland enjoy a remarkably mild climate, and snow is rare. Up here the wind is the main element; this is due to the land being closely surrounded by the sea. On the west side are the raging currents of the Atlantic, while in the east the North Sea roars in anger.

There are about a hundred islands altogether, and most are lonely places, the only inhabitants being sea-birds and seals. There are less than twenty inhabited islands, the largest of which is the mainland, called Zetland, the official name of Shetland.

In the streets and shops of Lerwick, the capital, you will meet Norwegians, Danes, Swedes, Russians, Germans, French, Poles, and every other European nationality that follows the sea. In Shetland there are more boats per head of population than cars, and almost everyone is a fisherman in one way or another, for the islands are situated in the middle of one

Four Guides carry lobster pots to the jetty, where a boat is waiting to take them out to sea

Guides Janet Johnson and Lyn Anderson try their hand at beachcombing

It is easy to make friends with the very tame "wild" Shetland ponies

The Guides go aboard for a trip to the island of Mousa

of the richest fishing-grounds in the world. Even richer may be the oil that is being brought ashore in growing volume and perhaps threatens some of the scenic beauty of the islands.

I met the Guides of the 1st Sandwick Company in Sandwick, a picture-postcard village strung along a wild, rocky shore. Most of the old Shetland families live in small crofting houses where the housewives knit the wool of the Shetland sheep into jumpers and sweaters that are known for their quality all over the world. In Shetland, sheep are not sheared in the normal way; the fleece is rooed —that is, simply pulled from the animal. I thought this was rather cruel, but one of the Guides explained that the animal feels no pain because the wool is loose in the spring and due to moult, and so comes away easily.

Sandwick is one of Shetland's best-known villages. It was from here that the Guides took a boat to the island of Mousa, famous for a strange stone tower called a broch, the best-preserved example of its kind in the world. The broch stands over forty feet high and has walls twenty feet thick. The amazing thing about it is that no mortar was used in its construction. Brochs were built by the Picts and served as homes for the people and shelter for their animals. The Guides climbed the staircase to the top of the tower.

Britain's last house, the northernmost dwelling on the land, at Skaw, on the island of Unst

The islands have their own distinct animals: Shetland sheep, sheepdogs, and, of course, the famous ponies, some of which you can see with the Guides on page 64. Shaggy, unkempt and wind-blown, the Shetland ponies are a familiar sight in most of the islands, but to see them at their best you have to visit the northern islands of Fetlar and Unst, the latter being Britain's northernmost island and home of thousands of seabirds. Contrary to popular belief, the ponies are not truly wild; they are very friendly. All are owned by crofters, though as they roam wherever they please they may give the impression that no one cares for them. In Sandwick lives the Lord-Lieutenant of Shetland, who owns some of the finest ponies in Shetland. We saw some of the animals being transported by boat to the island of Mousa.

One of the most memorable impressions the visitor to Shetlands brings away is the sight of these lovely furry ponies wandering amongst the heather with their soft-eyed, wide-awake foals against the background of the tempestuous North Sea.

My visit gave me a fascinating glimpse of Guiding in those far-north isles.

Patrol Camp Adventure

A Thrilling Guide Story in Pictures

What was he up to, Sally?
There was something alive in his basket. I heard it moving. Was he trapping something, do you think, Brenda?
Forgetting the trail in the excitement of the encounter, Brenda and Sally were overhauled by Jill and Monica.
There they are!
It's a fair cop!
Look - Sally, Jill, Monica - up over the wood!
It's a buzzard. Can you hear its mewing cry?
I thought buzzards were extinct.
There's a huge nest at the top of this tree.
They're jolly rare. What a thrill to see one.
After watching the buzzard until it flew out of sight, the Guides continued with their trail-laying. Early next morning they set off for a pre-breakfast hike.
You won't want any breakfast, Sally, eating chocolate.
It's because I do want breakfast that I'm eating. I'll never last out till we get back.
What on earth is that man doing? Look over there - he's dancing like a dervish
WHAT's a dervish, Brenda?
Gosh, look at all those birds darting and wheeling about above him.
The birds are mobbing him, aren't they?
There he goes. I'm certain it's the man Sally and I surprised yesterday.
I'd like to peep in his basket.
I know what you'd hope to find, Sally - grub.

The Guides came to the research station
NO ADMITTANCE BEWARE OF GUARD DOGS
The place must be in use already, judging by the security guards.
Thinking of trying to climb over, Brenda?
I vote we get back to camp. Somewhere a voice is calling, and I think it's calling breakfast.
Look - two buzzards - but what's up with them? They're behaving in an odd fashion.
They're too far away to see properly. I'll get my binoculars.
Nobody's parting me from my fried bread - not even buzzards.
I prefer breakfast to buzzards any day.
Something's wrong with the buzzards.
Let's run to the wood and see what's alarming them. I'll bet that wild man with the basket is somewhere around.
There's somebody climbing the tree.
I told you - it's the wild man.
He's robbing the nest.
So that's it - he's an egg-collector.
Leave the nest alone. Buzzards are protected birds. We shall report you if you take the eggs.
Great Scott, he's smashing the eggs!
This is awful!

Look, the male buzzard's attacking him!
Trying to beat off the fierce bird, the man lost his hold.
Look out -he's lost his hold!
He's falling!
The foliage broke your fall.
I don't think there are any bones broken.
Why, there's a pigeon in the basket!
The brute's going to kill another of my pigeons! I wanted to tear the nest to pieces. They're birds of prey – killers!
I've damaged my leg, I think.
We'll help you to Colonel Grice's house.
Where's Sally off to now?

You poor thing. You didn't have a chance when –hello, what's this? Why there's something fixed to your leg.
What's happened? Is the man injured?
He's hurt his leg, Colonel Grice nothing serious
He fell from a tree, Colonel Grice. He was trying to destroy the buzzard's eggs because his pigeons were being killed.
I found this on the pigeon the buzzard killed, Colonel Grice. It's a metal cylinder, and it's got a film inside it.
By George, microfilm showing the plan of the research station! No wonder he was mad when the buzzards destroyed his carrier pigeons.
After him – don't let him get away!
Good for you, girls! We'll get this chap under lock and key. Luckily, he can't run away after his fall. One of you nip over to the house and bring a couple of men. You've done a fine job in exposing this business.
We'd better change our name to the Buzzard Patrol – it was the buzzards that did it!
Please may we go back and finish our breakfast now?
Well, for once you've earned yours Sally.
A month later the Guides had a letter of thanks from the director of the atomic research station
The Director adds that despite the attack on the buzzards' eggs they have managed to hatch out a pair of young ones.
Well done, the buzzards!
And well done, the Blackbirds!

Trouble Trail

by Philip J. Randall

Five orange tents spread like late summer blooms about the small grass field.

"What a glorious spot for a campsite!" exclaimed Judith ecstatically. Judith was P.L. of the Squirrels.

"It certainly seems to have everything," agreed Anita, the Patrol Second.

"Everything" included the field sloping gently down to a brook, tall hedges on three sides to ensure privacy and to make a windbreak, and, a short distance away, a stretch of woodland inviting exploration. Beyond the western corner of the field a square tower and some roofs indicated the village that was to be the Guides' postal address.

"Tea up!" came the call from the kitchen area.

All the Guides scrambled to pick up their mugs and ran to where the Duty Patrol were waiting to fill them. Everybody agreed that setting up camp was inclined to promote a thirst that could only be quenched properly by slightly smoked tea.

On that point, the Guide Guider, Mrs. Parsons, observed to her Assistant, Miss Patrick, "I can't understand why people rave about China tea. To me it never fails to taste exactly like the tea we always have in camp—smoked."

After taking a preliminary sip of her tea, Mrs. Parsons put her mug down beside her on the grass and said, "This is only a refresher, Guides. You'll be having a proper meal at six o'clock, but I think this is a good time for me to be saying something about this camp. Most of you have been to camp before. For a few this is a first time. We shall find the countryside a lot different from the town in which we live, but I want you to remember that this is where the country people live. For Mr. Haddon, who has allowed us to camp here, this is his workshop. Respect it as such. Observe the Country Code. Leave gates as you find them. If they are shut, shut them after you. If they have been fastened open, leave them open. Above all, leave no litter. Hedges, ditches and fields are not intended to be refuse dumps."

"Are we allowed to go into the other fields?" Susan wanted to know.

"All the fields around here are farmed by Mr. Haddon. You have his permission to cross them, but don't do anything silly."

"I would rather go into the village. Is there a fish-and-chip shop?" asked Alison, who was a confirmed "townee". She had joined the Guides at a later age than most and this was her first camp.

"No fish-and-chip shop," laughed Mrs. Parsons, "but you may go into the village. Please tell me when you are going."

"What about the woods over there?" Judith asked. "They look very interesting."

"They are private property. The owner is Mr. Haddon. He grows most of the trees for timber. There is a saw-mill right in the middle of the woods and the place is out of bounds to the public except at weekends."

"Why only at weekends,

please, Mrs. Parsons?" Anita asked.

"For one thing, because the mill is not at work then. When the men are at work, carting and felling, they don't want crowds of people getting in the way. The only reason that the woods are open at all is that the County Naturalist Society have set up a nature trail there. We have been given permission to follow the nature trail on any day we wish. Each Patrol can follow the nature trail in turn, starting with the Squirrels."

On Monday morning, Mrs. Parsons handed over to Judith a board to which was clipped a number of papers.

"The printed sheet on the top is a plan of the nature trail," she explained. "Follow it round. At certain points you will find numbered posts. At each post read the appropriate notes. Make your own notes."

"What shall we say if anyone asks us what we are doing on private property," Debbie enquired nervously.

"No one should," Mrs. Parsons answered. "Everything is arranged. Your uniform is your passport." She gave the Squirrels details of how to reach the nature trail, and then the Patrol set off.

When the Guides reached the path leading to the nature trail, they saw that three boys had propped their bicycles against a wall, obviously waiting for one of their number inside the shop close by.

"Can anybody come?" a red-headed boy called cheekily.

Alison turned towards him, deliberately causing her long fair hair to swing out, and would have made some sort of a reply.

"Ignore them!" hissed Anita. "We don't want them following us."

The boys had their own ideas on that. They mounted their bicycles and pedalled after the Guides. They rode just behind them, making personal remarks. They seemed particularly taken with Alison. One of them insisted on calling her "Blondy".

Judith could see that Alison would have liked to linger to exchange pleasantries. She was glad when the Patrol reached the gate through which the nature trail was entered. The boys consulted among themselves, then turned and rode back in the direction of the village.

"That's got rid of that lot," Judith remarked. She led the way forward, keeping a lookout for the first marked post. Then she stopped, putting a hand behind her to halt the Patrol. "Look, a peacock!" she whispered.

"Where?" Alison whispered back. Her eyes followed Judith's pointing finger. "Oh, a butterfly!" she said disappointedly.

Judith giggled. "What did you expect to see—a bird? If I'd said 'Red Admiral' would you have looked for a high-ranking Russian sailor?"

By the time the Patrol reached Post Number Six, they had seen a woodmouse and several squirrels, gained a distant view of a woodpecker hammering at the bole of a tree, and identified a number of woodland flowers and grasses.

Post Number Six offered, according to the notes, a mixture of deciduous trees—lime, sycamore, oak and chestnut. Judith was knowledgeable enough to point out the differences in leaf-shapes. Sketches of these were duly transferred on to the clipboard by Debbie, who was rather good at drawing. The path at this point was narrow, and the Guides took up the whole width as they moved from tree to tree.

Judith was able to point out the differences in leaf-shapes

The youths hurriedly remounted and rode away

"Look out!" Anita shouted in sudden alarm.

The girls scattered into the trees as three cyclists rode bumpily past.

"Those boys again!" Judith muttered. "How did they get in?"

The village boys had in fact cycled back through the village and entered the woods by way of an unauthorised gate. Now that they had found the Guides they dismounted a short distance away. They propped their bicycles against a tree, called after "Blondy", made remarks, and laughed among themselves.

"Take no notice," Judith ordered, and continued to collect specimens of leaves to go with Debbie's sketches. The Patrol obeyed, with the exception of Alison. She insisted on looking towards the boys, encouraging them. They began swinging up and down on a branch, trying to attract the Guides' attention.

"Silly idiots! They're only showing off!" Anita said.

As she spoke, there was a loud crack. The branch, unable to bear the combined weight of the boys, crashed to the ground.

"Look out! The keeper's coming!" cried one of the boys, who picked themselves up hastily, remounted their cycles, and rode away.

As the Guides moved to the broken branch, the keeper came up. "So that's how you treat private property, is it?" he said gruffly.

"It was those village boys," explained Judith. "They swung on it."

"Helped by you," asserted the keeper. "You were all playing about together. I thought Girl Guides knew how to behave. You're the girls camping on Mr. Haddon's land, aren't you? Well, I shall report this to him. Now please get out of these woods. I'll show you the way."

Without heeding Judith's indignant protests, he shepherded the Guides along the path in the direction the boys had disappeared. When they came to a small handgate, he ushered them through and dropped the latch behind them.

"If Mr. Haddon takes my advice, he will ban all you campers from his woods from now on," he announced, and stumped away.

"What now?" Anita enquired.

"Go back to camp, I suppose," Judith replied, dismally.

"But not yet," said Anita, and pointed. "Those boys are still hanging about. We'd better let them go on before we move off."

The village boys were at the bottom of the sloping meadow into which the keeper had thrust the Guides. They had dismounted and were busy doing something in the wide brook that ran along the bottom of the meadow. Suddenly Judith cried out.

"The vandals! They're smashing up the footbridge over the stream! Come on, Squirrels—we'll scare 'em off!"

Anita chuckled as she saw the expression on the Patrol Leader's face. She knew that Judith was roused, and when Judith's blood was up there was trouble brewing for somebody!

Without further word, Judith raced off down the meadow, and the other Squirrels let out a whoop and followed. The village boys had ruined their morning and made trouble for the whole Company. They were delighted that Judith was leading them into battle against the enemy!

The "enemy", however, didn't wait to be challenged. When they saw the Guides racing towards them, they hurriedly remounted their bikes and rode away.

"Guilty consciences—that's what makes 'em run away!" panted Anita.

When the Guides reached the brook, they gazed in dismay at what they saw. The wooden footbridge over the brook had been all but torn up and broken in pieces. If, as seemed likely, it was in regular use by village people its loss would mean that a roundabout route would have to be taken by anyone wishing to go to and from the church and adjoining cottages that stood close to the gate through which the keeper had sent the Guides.

"Well, what a senseless thing to do!" said Susan, in disgust.

"This is what happens when youths haven't got anything to occupy themselves with," remarked Debbie.

"I don't like telling tales," said Anita, "but I do think we ought to report this to the police and describe the boys who did it."

"We could do that," agreed Judith, "but we could do something else—something more useful."

"You mean, try to repair the bridge?" said Alison doubtfully.

"We could have a shot at it. We're shut out of the nature trail, and we shan't be expected back at camp yet, so why not have a bash at repairing the footbridge? At the same time, we could clear up the litter that picnickers have left over the weekend. How about it, Squirrels?"

The rest of the Patrol enthusiastically agreed with the proposal. Under Judith's direction they set to work to retrieve the pieces of the broken bridge.

"What this bridge needs," said Judith briskly, "is some really workmanlike Guide lashing. Two volunteers, please, to run back to camp for rope and anything else that might come in handy for repairing the bridge!"

Susan and Anita volunteered and raced off. While they were gone, Judith and the others worked at getting the bridge into one piece again. By the time Anita and Susan returned they were ready to secure the bridge pieces with lashings. While they worked on the bridge, Susan and Debbie gathered up the litter left lying about by untidy picnickers.

"Now we'll set fire to it," said Debbie. "Here's a patch of ground where somebody has had a fire and burnt all the turf, so we'll put the rubbish here."

"How do we burn it?" asked Alison, joining them. "I don't suppose anybody has got any matches, have they?"

Nobody had.

"Try rubbing two sticks together," suggested Anita humorously.

"I've got a better idea," said Angela. She took off her glasses. "This may not be as quick as lighting with a match, but with patience it might work."

She held her glasses up to focus the sun's rays on to a piece of paper. Soon she was able to blow gently on the red-edged hole she produced; then she cried out triumphantly, "That's it!" and dropped the flaming paper on to the heap of litter.

"Hurray!" cried the Squirrels together—and then looked round in surprise.

"Hurray!" said a deep voice, and to their astonishment they realised that it came from the keeper, who was standing in the coppice adjacent to the footbridge and had evidently been quietly watching their activities.

"Oh!" exclaimed Judith.

"I take back all I said," said the keeper. "I owe you an apology. If you go to the trouble of clearing up other folk's litter you can't be the kind of girls who break down trees. What's happened to the little bridge you're repairing?"

"Those boys who swung on the branch along the nature trail smashed it up," Judith told him. "We thought we might as well do the villagers a good turn as we had nothing much to do, and repair the bridge as best we could. It isn't exactly perfect," she admitted, "but at least it will let people cross the stream until a stronger bridge can be put up."

"It seems to me you've made a very good job of it," said the keeper. "I'll see that another one is made as soon as it can be managed, but in the meantime I'm sure your repair will hold up. Thanks a lot to you all. Needless to say, I'll let Mr Haddon know that the Girl Guide campers can be relied on to respect his property, and of course you're at liberty to go back on the nature trail, if you've a mind to do so. As for those louts, I'll make it my business to find out who they are and drop a word in the right quarters about them."

"Thank you," said Judith, and the Guides gave a muted cheer.

"A pretty satisfactory ending, I think you'll agree," remarked Anita, as the keeper left.

"All I hope," said Judith, "is that our lashings will stand the test of heavyweight villagers crossing by the bridge. I should hate to think they'd give anybody a ducking."

"Unless it's those horrid boys," said Alison.

"I like that!" exclaimed Susan. "You were the one that encouraged them, Alison."

"I vote we send Alison on to the bridge for that!" said Debbie, chuckling. "If it gives way she'll get a ducking."

"All right," said Alison. "Watch me!" She ran on to the footbridge and across, then back again—and the bridge held firm.

"If it'll take Alison's weight," said Judith unkindly, "we need have no fear for anyone in the village. Come on—back to the nature trail!"

"I'm sure we shall enjoy it more now that we've done our day's good turn," said Judith. "Eh, Squirrels?"

The Squirrels agreed.

'Pick the Pictures'

Prize Competition

Win a New Bike and £50

First, put the six delightful pictures on pages 78 and 79 in the order in which you like them. For example, if you like **F** best you put **F** as number 1, the letter of your next choice as number 2, and so on down to number 6. Whatever your age you have as much chance as anyone else of winning the wonderful prize of a new bike for yourself and £50 for your Company.

The Editor has made his choice. If your first choice agrees with his, you will gain three points; if your second agrees with his, you will gain two points; for each of the others that agrees, one point will be awarded. The competitor with the most points will win the grand double prize. Something of equal value to the bike can be chosen, if preferred.

Now think of a good, pithy caption for each picture and write it down clearly in the space provided overleaf. Perhaps the whole Patrol could put their heads together to produce catchy captions. Give plenty of thought to the captions, because they will be taken into account if there are competitors with the same number of points.

Post your entry form to "PICK THE PICTURES" PRIZE COMPETITION, PURNELL BOOKS, BERKSHIRE HOUSE, QUEEN STREET, MAIDENHEAD, SL6 1NF, to arrive not later than March 31, 1980. The winner will be notified as soon as possible after this date. Entries from Guides in all countries are accepted.

"PICK THE PICTURES" COMPETITION ENTRY FORM

Just put the picture's letter in the order of your choice	
	My name is ....
	My address is ....
	....
	....
1....................	.... **My age is**......
2....................	**My Company is** ....
3....................	....
4....................	**My Guider's name and address is** ....
5....................	....
6....................	....

The winner of the 1978 prize competition was Rachel Haskell of the 1st Cippenham Company, Slough.

ANSWERS

MAP-READING QUIZ (p. 5):

1 Whether they have a tower, a spire, or neither; **2** bench marks used by the Ordnance Survey in surveying; **3** the boundaries of national parks are marked by a yellow line; **4** heights are given in metres, but the contour lines are at 50ft. intervals; **5** whether they can be used by vehicles (Ferry V) or only by passengers on foot (Ferry F); **6** by crossed swords with the date below; **7** the low and high water marks; **8** the names are printed on a blue shaded panel; **9** those that are always open are shown by NT in red, those with restricted opening are shown by NT in blue; **10** by a line with 'V's along it. On first series they were alternate, but on second series they are all below the line:

SCAVENGER HUNT (p. 51): 1-straw, 2-feathers, 3-stone, 4-furze, 5-water, 6-worm, 7-grass, 8-nest, 9-thorn, 10-moss

MESSAGE IN TIME (p. 51): Use the semaphore alphabet. Message: NEGLECT CAN BE SERIOUS

POTTY PLANTS (p. 77):

Mint, blackberries, gooseberries

NAME THE COUNTRIES (p. 77):

A-Egypt, B-Russia (U.S.S.R.), C-America (U.S.A.), D-Canada, E-Scotland

MORSE CODE MESSAGE (p. 58):

Don't look at the ground, But up and around. Overhead there's a bough, So jump for it now, Then swing into the tree, Where you'll surely find me.

PICTURE JIGSAW (p. 77):

Bluetit

CODES, SIGNS, SIGNALS (p. 58):

1. Very.
2. Yellow.
3. White.
4. Electric Telegraph.
5. Hotel.
6. Lamps.
7. Semaphore.
8. Echo.
9. Orange.
10. Erase.
11. Ensign.
12. N.C.
13. Conical.
14. Lifeguards.
15. Starboard.
16. Dangerous.
17. S O S.

"I thought there'd be an automatic dishwasher"

"Do you make fitted groundsheets?"

Write your captions here

A —

B —

C —

D —

E —

F —

The winner of the 1979 prize competition was Julie Anne Partridge of the 1st Yetminster Company, Sherborne, Dorset

PUZZLE PICTURES

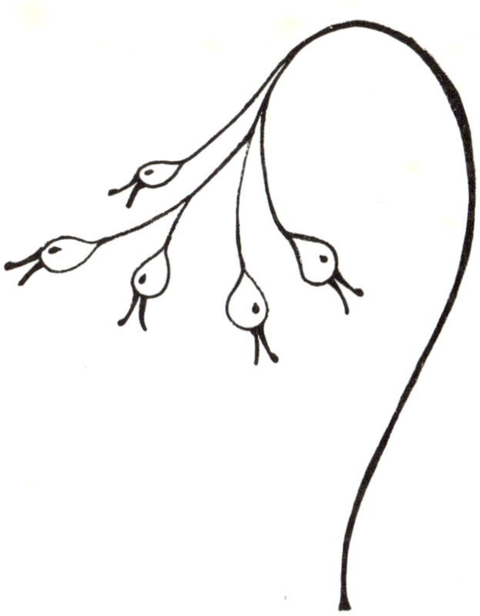

Potty Plants

Can you put a name to each of these three "potty plants"?

Name the Countries

What countries are represented by these flags, which are not the real national flags?

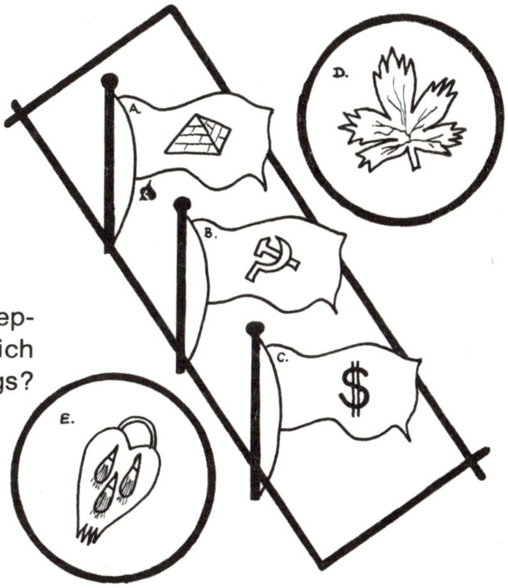

Picture Jigsaw

To find out what Patrol bird is represented here, copy each drawing on the left into the frame with the corresponding number on the right.

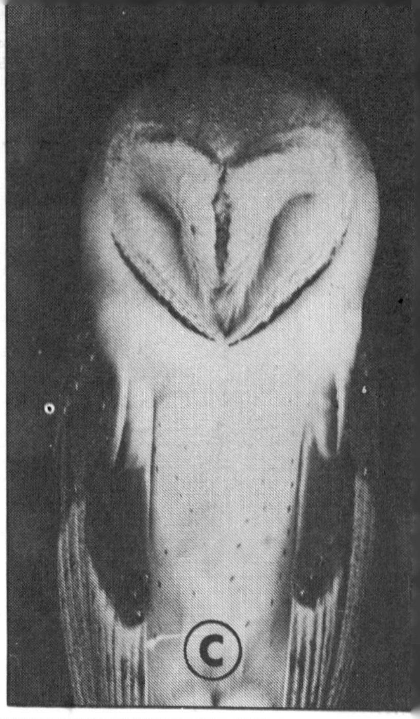

'Pick the Pictures' £100 Prize Competition